THE NATIONAL CURRICULUM
AND THE PRIMARY SCHOOL

Bedford Way Series
Published by Kogan Page in association with the Institute of Education, University of London

The National Curriculum and the Primary School Jeni Riley (ed.) *English and the National Curriculum* Ken Jones (ed.) *History in the National Curriculum* Richard Aldrich (ed.) *Quality Assurance and Accountability in Higher Education* Cari Loder (ed.) *Britain and a Single Market Europe: Prospects for a common school curriculum* Martin McLean *Financial Support for Students: grants, loans or graduate tax?* Maureen Woodhall (ed.) *Looking, Making and Learning: Art in the primary school* Anthony Dyson (ed.) *Personal and Social Education: philosophical perspectives* Patricia White (ed.) *Reforming Religious Education: the religious clauses of the 1988 Education Reform Act* Edwin Cox and Josephine M Cairns *The National Curriculum* Denis Lawton and Clyde Chitty (eds).

Contents

First published in 1992

Kogan Page Limited
120 Pentonville Road
London N1 9JN

© Institute of Education, 1992

British Library Cataloguing in Publication Data

A CIP record for this book is available from the British Library

ISBN 0 7494 0642 9

Typeset by Paul Stringer, Watford
Printed and bound in Great Britain by
Biddles Ltd, Guildford and Kings Lynn

THE BEDFORD WAY SERIES

THE NATIONAL CURRICULUM AND THE PRIMARY SCHOOL

Springboard or Straitjacket?

Edited by
JENI RILEY

Contributors:
Tricia Connell, Andrew Brown, Jane Savage,
Marilyn Metz, Caroline Heal, Roy Prentice,
Janet Sparkes, Barry Fry, June Boyce-Tillman

KOGAN
PAGE

Published in association with
The Institute of Education, University of London

Notes on Contributors

Jeni Riley, the editor, is course tutor for the Primary Postgraduate Certificate of Education at the Institute of Education. She has taught infants and been an advisory teacher in Oxfordshire. Currently, she is engaged in research into literacy and the first year of school.

Andrew Brown has taught in primary schools in North and East London. He is presently a lecturer in primary education and mathematics education at the Institute of Education, University of London.

Tricia Connell at the time of writing was a lecturer in primary education at the Institute of Education, having previously taught in primary schools in Nottinghamshire.

Barry Fry is a senior lecturer in human movement and physical education at King Alfred's College, Winchester. Before his present post, he taught in a middle school in Suffolk.

Caroline Heal is a lecturer in primary education at the Institute of Education. She leads and co-ordinates the humanities module on the PGCE and has taught in the OU.

Marilyn Metz has taught in infant schools in Haringey and was part of an early research project on Logo with early years children. She is currently a lecturer in primary education at the Institute of Education.

Roy Prentice is a senior lecturer and chairperson of the Department of Art and Design at the Institute of Education. Previously, he was responsible for all aspects of art and design education in primary and secondary education as County Art Adviser in East Sussex.

Jane Savage has taught in primary schools in North London and has held an advisory post for science education. She is currently working on a

research project on school development and is also a lecturer in primary
education at the Institute of Education.

Janet Sparkes is Senior Lecturer and Head of the Movement Studies
Department at King Alfred's College, Winchester, and previously has
taught in secondary, primary and special schools in Sussex and Hamp-
shire.

June Boyce-Tillman has wide experience of primary schools in London
and taught music on the postgraduate course at the Institute of Education.
She is currently a senior lecturer in music education at King Alfred's
College, Winchester.

Introduction
The National Curriculum and the Primary School

Jeni Riley

In September 1989, a state-controlled curriculum was introduced to the new school pupils starting their education. For the first time in English and Welsh history, English, mathematics and science, the core subjects of the National Curriculum, were taught to children entering the age-phase 5 to 7, Key Stage 1.

The purpose of this publication is to give the considered reaction of some professionals to the National Curriculum now in place in the primary schools. The book is written by a team of initial teacher educators who are primary generalists (with one exception). They have interests in, and enthusiasm for, the different areas about which they have written, rather than a curriculum specialist focus. The views that they express concern the primary school and its ethos of cross-curricular teaching. This gives the chapters a broader perspective. The individual chapters are written with themes in mind but with interesting and different emphases.

The impact of the core subjects – English, mathematics and science – on the primary curriculum in the last two years will be critically evaluated. Design and technology, only a year after implementation, and history, geography, art, music and physical education, on which National Curriculum documents have more recently been issued, will be handled differently. The focus of these chapters will be on the documents and their relationships with current research and thinking on the best of primary practice. Issues of assessment, albeit a changing scene, will be addressed in this introduction. This is our considered view of the National Curriculum as we experience it through our work with students and teachers in primary schools.

We write with a spirit of optimism. A National Curriculum might arguably provide an opportunity for greater equality for all children and present a challenge to primary schools to deliver the broader and more rigorous curriculum. The aim to bring the poorer schools up to the level of the exemplars of good practice is laudable. The general intentions of the National Curriculum (DES, 1987) have met with professional approval. These principles will make it possible to achieve greater uniformity and continuity within and between primary schools.

Importantly, for the first time in primary education, there is to be a clear entitlement of curricular content for all children. The National Curriculum and related assessment arrangements aim to ensure that all pupils study a broad and balanced range of subjects throughout their schooling. The setting of clear objectives over a full ability range should enable children to achieve their potential. Her Majesty's Inspectorate (HMI) have consistently reported in national surveys a worrying under-achievement of many pupils. There is now the aim that all children, regardless of sex, ethnic origin and geographical location, will have access to broadly the same curriculum.

The implementation of the National Curriculum in the primary school is at different stages for different areas. The core subjects of English, mathematics and science have been in place for two years, design and technology for over 12 months. For this reason, and given the way in which the National Curriculum is structured, we shall be considering its implementation subject by subject in the succeeding chapters. But learning for young children is holistic and not in separate subject entities. For this reason we believe that we should continue to teach in an integrated and traditionally primary manner in school. The fragmentation of the primary curriculum into subjects is reflected in the way that this book is structured. The extent to which the primary curriculum has been affected by this potential hazard will be discussed in the individual chapters.

There are risks, then, as well as opportunities. We are concerned about the threat to primary ideology posed by a curriculum structured around rigid subject areas. We are adamant that the disparate curricular demands are putting pressure on the generalist teacher. The reading and absorption alone of the Statutory Orders for English, mathematics, science, history, geography and technology and the non-statutory guidelines has been a massive task for staff in the primary school. Small wonder that there was barely a ripple of interest at the appearance of the Interim Reports for music, art and PE. The next step, namely to incorporate the National Curriculum into primary philosophy, with holistic learning at its heart, has been a greater challenge. This has been all the more difficult for small schools. The impact on schools, teachers and, crucially, the children of the assessment procedures will be addressed later in this chapter. Another major criticism to be aired will be evidence of the lack of early-years specialists on the various working parties. This has created anomalies in the Levels 1 to 3 of Key Stage 1 in English for example.

These and other worrying issues aside, the main thrust of our argument is positive. It is first necessary to be aware of the background to the introduction of the National Curriculum.

The background

The social, economic and educational context from which came the Education Reform Act 1988 dates back to the early 1970s. The Black Papers of 1975 and 1977 followed a wave of public concern about educational standards. The eleven-plus had widely been abolished and primary education broadened and changed with the influence of the Plowden Report in 1967. Despite HMI surveys that claimed discovery learning and a child-centred, integrated curriculum were not as prevalent as the critics believed, James Callaghan demanded more accountability in education during his Ruskin College speech in 1976. Many LEAs responded by reintroducing standardized tests in reading, maths and (in some cases) verbal reasoning. However, little positive use was made of the results of this monitoring and concern continued. In the late 1970s the Assessment and Performance Unit was established with the brief to evaluate the efficiency of teaching and learning within and between schools. Whilst much valuable information has been gathered by the APU, it has not enabled *schools* to be evaluated on performance indicators or 'educational standards' to be monitored. There are many complex reasons for this. The two main ones are that curriculum changes make test results over five years meaningless and that the tests themselves become outdated.

Through the early 1980s, systems of testing, monitoring and school self-evaluation continued. But political attention became more focused on the perceived necessity to evaluate teacher efficiency, to raise 'standards' and to increase competition between schools. This concern to raise standards was across the political parties and was partly derived from Britain's poor standing in the world market-place. From within the profession itself, HMI, continuously it seemed, had been critical of the 'patchiness' found in the provision offered by primary schools.

The National Curriculum and linked assessment, stated the DES, would *prove* to be an acceptable way of *raising* standards (DES, 1987). A curriculum devised by the Government-selected Working Parties and taught to all pupils from 5 to 16 would be introduced. All children of 7,

11, 14, and those not assessed via GCSE at 16, were to be assessed using tests and activities derived from the National Curriculum. This is a very different model from that devised for the APU Attainment Targets, which is the description of knowledge and understanding to be acquired and is divided into ten levels of performance. The Levels of Attainment of the three core curriculum subjects were to be monitored both by teacher assessment and statutory Standard Assessment Tasks. In 1990 it was decided that the foundation subjects were to be assessed solely. Formative assessment by the teacher is expected to provide the basis from which to devise the next teaching programme for the child. It aims to provide information on the child's level of functioning in the specific Programme of Study, which is valuable for the teacher, school and nationally. This is the claim.

This central control of the curriculum, starting for the first time at school entry, is achieved by the dual effect of the introduction of a National Curriculum, its Programmes of Study and the assessment of the Attainment Targets of the content. Secondary schools have always had the external influence of the examination syllabus. Now the primary school is to be equally constrained.

Assessment

Any consideration of the impact of the National Curriculum in primary schools has to include the implications of assessment. Curriculum and assessment are interrelated aspects of the 1988 Education Reform Act, and it is the provision for assessment which gives the curriculum measures their power.

Assessment has been used for several purposes. Caroline Gipps (1990) suggests that an understanding of the National Curriculum assessment can only be achieved by viewing development historically. Qualifying examinations for the medical and legal professions began in the early nineteenth century. Entry examinations for these professions and to university followed. The development of the intelligence tests at the beginning of this century led to the belief that individuals could be pre-selected for the type of education that most suited their intellectual capacity, and the eleven-plus was born. Children were thus separated into the academic and the less academic. The former were channelled into gaining entry into the professions by way of achieving O level and A level examinations. Much has been written and said about the inequity of such pre-determination of people at the age of 11.

In the last ten years, new developments in assessment have taken place, namely the GCSEs, graded assessment and profiles or records of achievement. It also needs to be stated that these have had the other effect of controlling curriculum content. The primary purpose of these assessments has been to improve pupil motivation, particularly in those who at present have poor employment prospects. Whether it has succeeded in this is arguable.

Following on from this it becomes clear that one of the aims of the National Assessment proposed in 1988 was to ensure that teachers taught the National Curriculum and taught it well. There is a sense of *deja vu* – the 'Revised Code' of 1860 was introduced for the same reasons, and to evaluate teacher effectiveness.

Assessment has many uses – screening, diagnosis, record keeping, feedback on performance, selection and certification among others. Which of these uses is it deemed that the National Curriculum will fulfil? Screening, traditionally, has been a way of identifying children in need of special help. It might be argued that the new procedures will achieve this. Diagnostic testing to identify strengths and weaknesses of the child has commonly been conducted by an educational psychologist, specialist or an advisory teacher. It is unlikely that this purpose will be fulfilled by the National Curriculum Assessment. Record keeping will be a benefit of the new assessment although it is unlikely to be sufficiently detailed in the early years of schooling. Other forms of record keeping will most likely need to be kept, such as the Primary Language Record – time and energy permitting!

The main function of the proposed forms of Teacher Assessment and Standard Assessment Tasks will be for feedback on performance. Children's results will indicate both their own progress and the teacher's success. This will be used to inform the next teaching stage as stated earlier. Results will also be used by teachers as the basis on which to discuss a child's progress with parents. This is the first time primary teachers will have to be so explicit regarding their pupils' level of functioning and it is likely to raise some anxiety, certainly initially. Much detailed explanation of the complex system will also be necessary in order to avoid merely confusing those not professionally involved.

The class results will be made available to governors, LEA officials and parents. The aggregates of Key Stage 2 results are to be published. This intentional by-product of the assessment will ensure that schools will be more accountable for the education they offer their pupils both individually and collectively. Governing bodies will be in a position to evaluate a school's performance, taking into account local circumstances, by a national yardstick.

What is not clear is the extent to which these results will be used in teacher appraisal. Certainly the opportunity to use league tables of schools, on the basis of national assessment results, as performance indicators for schools is obvious. Professionals need to be vociferous about how dangerous this practice could be. It would narrow the criteria by which schools should be evaluated unacceptably. Also, the test results have no validity without an adjustment for socio-economic status and educational level of parents of the school intake. It is possible, through a sophisticated statistical technique, to adjust for factors well known to disadvantage children (Goldstein, 1987). As yet it is not clear whether it is envisaged that use will be made of this technique in the national assessment data. The Task Group on Assessment and Testing (TGAT) Report made no effort to enlighten us. The purpose of the new assessment procedures is not claimed to be selective. It may well be a result.

The Circular Number 3 produced by the National Curriculum Council (1989) suggested that the most effective organization of classes may not be by age. The implication is that children will be grouped by ability and selected through the results of the assessment. To be positive, this may lessen the incidence of poor 'match' in primary classes referred to by HMI (1978) and Bennett et al (1984). Gipps (1990) suggests that we will see able children going through levels more quickly (and it was about these children that HMI expressed most concern) and that, inevitably, younger brighter children will be working with older, less able children. The effect of this on the self-image of very young children is still unclear. A proud characteristic of British primary schools has been the orchestrated non-competitive atmosphere. The supportive ethos of the nurturing of each pupil is one that we would wish to uphold and to which national assessment poses a threat (DES, 1989, para. 74). Both the assessment arrangements and the content of the National Curriculum are giving concern to educationalists and a reconsideration of the teaching mode in the older years of the primary school (Alexander, 1991).

Kenneth Baker, former Secretary of State for Education, unpersuaded by primary educators' rhetoric, is quoted in the *Daily Telegraph* as saying:

> It has become rather unfashionable to give tests to children today because there is a belief that they segregate the winners from the losers... Parents know that approach was bogus. *(9/2/87)*

It will be a decade or more before the parents and the professionals will be able to evaluate the educational progress of the 7-year-old 'losers'. Barker-Lunn's work (1970) might lead us not to be sanguine of their success once so labelled.

The assessment procedures will not be used for certification although they could conceivably be used to add standard information to profiles and records of achievement.

Set in a 'value for money' climate, it has been attempted to show the ways in which national assessment will increase competitiveness between children and between schools and also seeks to address the issue of teacher and school accountability. Sheer volume of work threatens the valued characteristics of the primary school such as the ethos and the relationship between teacher and child. A small scale study (Barbara Hull, 1990) carried out last year demonstrated that infant teachers are feeling very pressured which makes them irritable with the pupils. This was prior to teacher assessment and Standard Assessment Tasks arriving on the scene. Gipps (1990) claims that an infant teacher with 30 children may have to deal with over 8,000 pieces of information over the SAT testing period. For the junior teacher at the end of Key Stage 2 there will be more. But, professionals will meet the demands made on them at Key Stage 2 as it has been seen that they have at Key Stage 1. As they work with the ten National Curriculum areas and the assessment, they will need to hold to a firm belief in the ways that children learn effectively.

Research data now emerging from the ESRC funded project, 'National Assessment in Primary Schools: An Evaluation' by Caroline Gipps, Bet McCallum, Shelley McAlister and Margaret Brown (1991), is shedding light on the implementation of SATs in schools. Caroline Gipps and her colleagues have studied the impact of the assessment on 32 classes in four areas of the country. An interesting picture is emerging.

Clearly, the extra work load, and changes in re-organization for the classes, and in some cases schools, is causing stress. Organizationally, those schools which have vertical grouping in place found the SAT period less problematic. Stress was a major theme and was reported as being evident at some level by 25 out of 31 headteachers. Support, from within the schools, for the Year 2 teacher varied enormously but was not linked to the level of the reported observed stress.

Eight of the 32 were described as low stress schools. Five of these were vertically grouped with few children in Year 2, and in three of the schools the heads were moderators. It may well have been the experience of the heads which gave teachers the confidence in organizing their groups of children. Moreover having 12 Year 2 children to assess has to be easier than 28.

The effect on the children is less clearly defined by the data. Great efforts were made to protect the SAT children from the 'test' situation. In spite of this some were upset and on occasions the assessment was abandoned. Greater concern in the project was expressed about the non-SAT children who were working under the jurisdiction of an ancillary helper or parent. Many teachers felt guilty about the comparatively low challenge in the activities set up for them.

Caroline Gipps and her colleagues found that, while initial reaction to the experience was that 15 teachers said they had learnt nothing from the assessment, during the lengthy interviews that followed, it transpired that 'virtually all our schools found that they had learnt something from the SAT experience'. One headteacher summed up the overall value by saying:

> It has certainly taught the staff much about organization, teamwork, forward thinking, planning, assessing, teaching and last but not least enjoyment.

It seems then that the early conclusions of the project are that the teachers felt that, whilst there had been benefits, there had been little insight gained from the actual assessment aspect over and above the value of close observation. This might indicate that teacher assessment is as valuable as a standard assessment. Broadfoot et al (1991) corroborate that there is evidence that teachers are becoming more skilled and flexible in integrating teaching and assessment. Also they are more confident in the predictive nature of their assessment.

The signs are that the Government is not likely to abandon Standard Assessment Tasks simply because they do not tell the teacher anything novel; rather it will be because they are too complex and time consuming (*Times Educational Supplement*, Sept 1991).

The move towards paper and pencil tests as a solution to the complexity is argued against by Resnick and Resnick (1991). Standardized testing has been criticized for being based on faulty learning-theory assumptions. The antithesis is seen by Shepard (1991) as authentic assessment: '...authentic assessment which supports good teaching by not requiring teachers to redirect attention away from important concepts, in-depth projects, and the like.'

Caroline Gipps asserts that the 1991 Key Stage 1 SATs were designed on this model of assessment, whatever the shortcomings. The tasks were both activity- and process-based and could be used consistently with good infant practice. The prospect of a move away from the latter to narrow pen and pencil tests is horrifying.

It is stated that the National Curriculum offers greater curriculum opportunity for all children (DES, 1987). It would be a grave omission in an opening chapter not to consider whether this claim will be fulfilled for all groups of pupils. It is well documented that there are different patterns of intellectual functioning in boys and girls (for a succinct summary of the literature see Harvey Goldstein's (1988) report for the Equal Opportunities Commission). Research findings show that ethnic minorities underachieve also for complex and interrelated reasons (Rutter et al, 1974; Essen and Ghodsian, 1979; Mabey, 1981; Rampton, 1981; Swann, 1985; Eggleston et al, 1986). The Infant School Study (Tizard et al, 1989) showed that although Afro-Caribbean girls and boys scored as well at the end of nursery as the white boys and girls, by the end of Reception Class the Afro-Caribbean boys were doing less well than the three other groups (ie black girls, white boys and white girls). This effect was discovered in secondary schools also (Smith and Tomlinson, 1989). Hypotheses have been generated that the reasons for this might be teacher bias and expectation of ability on behaviour grounds.

Within the minefield of cultural difference and alienation and of the frequently linked low socio-economic status and poor educational opportunity, we have now an assessment system that not only militates against bilingual learners but makes virtually no provision for them.

The TGAT Report (DES, 1988) simply recommends that 'where necessary and practical, assessments be carried out in pupils' first language and that assessment items be reviewed for bias in respect of gender and race' (Gipps, 1990). It seems that there is much work to be done both in initial training and in-service support to ensure that teacher stereotyping of groups of children is addressed.

The ESRC Project (Gipps et al, 1991) seems tentatively to suggest that bilingual learners were performing better than teachers had predicted on the SATs. This might well prove to be one of the more positive aspects of the experience.

Integration and the National Curriculum

The National Curriculum has been conceived in subject areas but the primary curriculum, endorsing the liberal-romantic tradition, has been taught through the topic approach. The Plowden Report (Central Advisory Council of Education, 1967) saw this way of work as being:

...designed to make good use of the interest and curiosity of children, to minimize the notion of subject matter being rigidly compartmentalized and to allow the teacher to adopt a consultative, guiding, stimulating role rather than a purely didactic one. *(Para. 540)*

Topic work is promoted enthusiastically more recently by Stephen Rowland (1984) in his model of 'interpretative teaching' in which teaching and learning are seen as a dynamic interaction between teacher and pupils. In Rowland's model, sometimes the teacher, sometimes the children might be the stimulus, or initiator. The teacher supports, guides and extends the learning and so is the facilitator.

Topic work, whilst at its best exciting and valuable, can, at its worst, degenerate to the point where the 'poorest readers do little other than copy statements or cut-out pictures' (Maxwell, 1977). And Eric Bolton, the former Chief Senior Inspector, criticized the erstwhile Inner London Education Authority in the following terms: 'The main area of weakness is on topic work. In common with this type of work in the country at large, teachers leave too much to chance in their planning and are unclear about their objectives and opportunities for learning that need to be exploited. As a result the work is often over prescribed, undemanding and lacking rigour.'

Kerry and Eggleston (1988) identify perhaps the most serious weakness as the lack of evaluation, monitoring and recording of children's progress. Perhaps the implementation of the National Curriculum will correct these serious flaws of content, continuity, progression, and rigour, provided primary teachers are able to teach in a cross-curricular way and still adequately cover the content of the Statutory Orders. Teachers are working to achieve both these ends.

Stephen Ward (1990) believes that, whilst the Rowland model is no longer possible, primary schools must resist the temptation to pre-plan all their work to fit completely the Attainment Targets to be covered. Ward states that teachers and children will only genuinely be committed to topics they own: '...if the unified topic which is of interest and importance to the children is at the centre of the curriculum, any additional "routine" or directed work necessary to complete the comprehensive curriculum will be readily accepted by the children when they know that the teacher shares their overall excitement about learning.'

It may well be that curriculum overload rather than adherence to primary ideology has made schools cling to a cross-curricular thematic approach. It could also be that as teachers become more familiar with the documentation, the Programmes of Study and Attainment Targets, the theme, as Ward proposes, will more often become the starting point rather than the reverse.

Integration is logically achieved when addressing the four Attainment Targets of English, speaking, listening, reading and writing. These aspects of written and oral language clearly support and permeate every aspect of the taught curriculum. Integration is not so easy to achieve when conducting assessment. The piloting of the Standard Assessment Tasks has highlighted that the observational and analytical skills of assessment that the class teacher needs demand a single subject focus.

The debate has been moved on further by the report of the 'Three Wise Men' (Alexander, Rose and Woodhead, 1992). This discussion paper is the result of the enquiry into primary teaching called for by Secretary of State for Education, Kenneth Clarke, in November 1991.

Alexander et al state that they doubt whether the demands of the National Curriculum *can* adequately be met by the generalist primary teacher. Four teaching roles are suggested: the generalist; the generalist/consultant, who provides cross-school co-ordination of particular subjects; the semi-specialist, who teaches a particular subject but also has a general class teacher role; and the full-time specialist. The operation of some or a mixture of these models of primary teaching is their solution to the increased demands that the National Curriculum makes on the subject expertise of teachers.

As regards pedagogy, the report makes a strong case for more subject teaching and, where appropriate, whole class teaching. Despite the danger of pitching to the middle level, whole class teaching is associated with '...higher order questioning, explanations and statements, and these in turn correlate with higher levels of pupil performance.'

Many valuable opportunities are lost by adopting too narrow a focus. A working knowledge of the National Curriculum documents reveals the overlap of subject areas so it makes sense from an economy of time point of view to cover work simultaneously where possible with a theme or topic approach. Scientific understanding is deepened by close observation and drawing of natural phenomena. Art as a tool for learning in this way is discussed in chapter 6.

June Tillman in her chapter feels that the close link between music and dance has been largely ignored in the physical education documents. A child listens to music and responds with his or her whole body to music through dance. Teachers with specialist knowledge and familiar with the documents are able to exploit the rich potential for many examples of such overlap. The essence of gifted primary teaching lies in this ability as much now as it has in the past.

Primary teachers' initial and in-service education

The National Curriculum is now fully incorporated into initial teacher education courses, both in the form of being part of the students' awareness of content in planning and considering work for the classroom. Also, courses have to meet the curricular demands made on the students' subject knowledge. This makes excessive demands on taught hours, particularly on the postgraduate one-year courses. 'Issue in Education' courses are the frequent casualty of time re-allocation. The cynical teacher educators amongst us feel that this is an intentional by-product of the National Curriculum. The subject permutation demands of information technology competence and economic awareness also erode thinking and reading time on courses.

Initial teacher education has to respond also to the CATE stipulation that subject or curriculum co-ordinators are trained on PGCE courses. It is envisaged by the DES that the mathematics graduate will become the mathematics co-ordinator in school after a few years' teaching experience. Sadly, many degree specialisms do not transfer so readily to the primary curriculum.

The National Curriculum is making huge inroads into the budgets of LEAs, and, now, schools themselves, in terms of in-service training of teachers. Teachers have needed great support to teach the core science and this has led, as we shall see in chapter 4, to an over-emphasis on this subject area. Now it is envisaged that the rigour demanded by the art, music and history and geography documents will need similar specialist in-service training.

This enhancement in the generalist teachers' understanding of the different specialist areas of the primary curriculum is the challenge of the National Curriculum. Alexander et al and Her Majesty's Inspectorate are dubious about whether most primary teachers are capable of delivering the curriculum as it is intended. The many documents add up to an awesome professional task, but one that most primary teachers will willingly undertake provided the general public, parents and pupils are prepared to place their trust in them.

References
Alexander, R. (1991) *Primary Education in Leeds.* School of Education, Leeds.
Alexander, R., Rose, J. and Woodhead, C. (1992) *Curriculum Organisation and Classroom Practice in Primary Schools – A Discussion Paper.* DES.

Barker-Lunn, J. (1970) *Streaming in the Primary School*. Windsor: NFER.

Bennett, H., Desforges, C., Cockburn, A. and Wilkinson, B. (1984) *The Quality of Pupil Learning Experiences*. London: Lawrence Erlbaum.

Broadfoot, P., Abbot, D., Croll, P., Osborn, M., Polland, A. and Towler, L. (1991) 'Implementing National Assessment: Issues for Primary Teachers.' *Cambridge Journal of Education*, 21, 2.

Central Advisory Council of Education (England) (1967) *Children and Their Primary Schools (The Plowden Report)*. London: HMSO.

DES (1987) *The National Curriculum 5–16: A Consultation Document*. DES/Welsh Office.

DES (1988) *National Curriculum: Task Group on Assessment and Testing: A Report*. DES/Welsh Office.

DES (1989) *The National Curriculum: From Policy to Practice*. DES/Welsh Office.

Eggleston, J. (1988) 'The New Educational Bill and Assessment - Some Implications for Black Children.' *Multicultural Teacher*, 6, 2.

Eggleston, J., Dunn, D., Anjali, M. and Wright, C. (1986) *Education for Some*. Stoke-on Trent: Trentham Books.

Essen, J. and Ghodsian, M. (1979) *The Children of Immigrants: School Performance*. New Community.

Gipps, C. (1990) *Assessment – A Teacher's Guide to the Issues*. Hodder & Stoughton.

Gipps, C., McCallum, B., McAlister, S. and Brown M. (1991) 'National Assessment at Seven: Some Emerging Themes.' In: Gipps, C.(ed.) *Developing Assessment for the National Curriculum*. (Bedford Way Series) London: Kogan Page.

Goldstein, H. (1987) *Multilevel Models in Educational and Social Research*. London: Charles Griffin & Co.

Goldstein, H. (1988) *National Testing and Equal Opportunities, Appendix to TGAT Report*. DES.

HMI (1978) *Primary Education in England: A Survey by HMI*. London: HMSO.

Hull, B. (1990) 'The National Curriculum: its effects on infant teachers and their practice.' *Tactyc Journal*, Autumn.

Kerry, T. and Eggleston, J. (1988) *Topic Work in the Primary School*. Routledge & Kegan Paul.

Mabey, C. (1981) *Black British Literacy: A Study of Reading Attainment of London Black Children from 8–15 years*. Education and Research.

Maxwell, J. (1977) *Reading Progress from 8–15*. Slough: NFER.

National Curriculum Council (1989) *Implementing the National Curriculum in Primary Schools*. Circular No. 3, NCC.

Resnick, L. and Resnick, D. (1991) 'Assessing the Thinking Curriculum: new tools for educational reform.' In: Gifford, B. and O'Connor, M. (eds) *Future Assessments: Changing Views of Aptitude, Achievement and Instruction*. Kluwer Academic Publishers.

Rampton (1981) *West Indian Children in Our Schools, (CMND 8273)*. London: HMSO.

Rowland, S. (1984) *The Enquiring Classroom*. Lewes: The Falmer Press.

Rutter, M., Yulk, W. and Berger, M. (1974) 'The Children of West Indian Migrants.' New Society.

Shepard, L. (1991) 'Interviews on Assessment Issues with Lorrie Shepard.' *Educational Researcher*, 20, 21 (March).

Smith, D. and Tomlinson, S. (1989) *The School Effect*. London Policy Studies, Institute of Education, University of London.

Swann, M. (1985) *Education for All, (CMND 9453)*. London: HMSO.

Times Educational Supplement, September 1991.

Tizard, B., Blatchford, P., Burke, J., Farquar, C. and Plewis, I. (1988) *Young Children at School in the Inner City*. Lawrence Erlbaum Associates.

Ward, S. (1990) *The Primary Core National Curriculum*. London: Cassell.

Chapter One
English: Meaning More, Not Less

Tricia Connell

In the National Curriculum, English is defined as a core subject which has two kinds of responsibility. First it is the standard language which all children are to learn; and second it is the medium for schooled learning in writing, reading, speaking and listening. The main components of the National Curriculum for English correspond, therefore, to categories which parents and teachers already understand, but which are now more explicitly defined in terms of what is to be learnt in school and how progress is to be assessed and measured.

What the long-term effects this sharper definition of the subject may have upon children's experience of language in primary schools has yet to be seen. Educationalists have been highly critical of the speed at which the Government has imposed the National Curriculum and has introduced procedures for its assessment without either serious consideration of the concerns raised by teachers or time allowed for research. The very use of the term English to describe and define all children's language experience in school conceals both the political and intellectual struggles which are involved in maintaining the dominance of a particular culture. It also glosses over the conceptual tangle which many non-specialist primary teachers, used to teaching language across the curriculum, have yet to address.

Nevertheless, many teachers have assigned these initial, fundamental concerns to recent history and looked with uneasy relief at the statutory order for English. They have been relieved that it both encapsulates some current and successful practices related to children becoming readers and learning to write and it makes explicit the critical place of talk in children's learning. The National Curriculum for English, as it stands at present, therefore, does not reduce teaching to the inculcation of literacy skills and formal grammar as educationalists once feared. On the contrary there are aspects which could serve as a reasonable starting point for ongoing curriculum development.

Unfortunately, the present generation of children in state schools may have to bear the brunt of the inconsistencies. Profound concerns remain on at least three counts. Firstly, there are problems in mapping a complex interactive subject like English across ten levels for purposes of assessment and testing. It is feared that the delivery of a package of many arbitrarily determined and loosely related practices within a rigid and prescriptive framework for the purposes of assessment may seriously restrict children's access to a broad language curriculum.

Another major concern is the degree of specification used to define and separate affective and cognitive aspects of learning language. Experienced teachers are well aware that, for instance, content and form in young children's writing are often inextricably linked. The danger is that those unspecified, but no less critical aspects of language, will be given less time and attention in schools due to excessive concern for quantifiable outcomes at specific stages. Thus there may well be a lowering of children's achievement in dramatic and visual modes of language and, likewise, in the development of their personal, authentic and committed writing. Should this happen, then it is not difficult to see how much of the life and interest in learning in primary school will be lost to the very children who have most to gain from a broad language curriculum. Children who are bidialectical and bilingual, children who have language experiences which differ widely from the language and culture of the school, will be more disadvantaged by a reduction in opportunity to explore and articulate their knowledge across a full range of language modes.

The imposition and political control of a model of standard English which all children must learn, and all teachers are required by law to teach, is yet another issue which remains unresolved. Never before has the use of standard English been made so explicit in the content of the curriculum and the procedure for its assessment at all levels of schooling.

The sad irony in the National Curriculum is that the components of the statutory order for English, whilst being familiar, have also been defined in ways which may be difficult to recognize as fully as current practice makes desirable. To wait for the future to unravel the web of inconsistencies which are already apparent is untenable for those of us who wish to ensure that the actual and potential achievement of all children in English continues to rise. Instead we will be wise to examine critically both established orthodoxies and innovative practices which are related to language in school in order to identify the different futures that are possible. We may then select the one which is most relevant and nurture it.

This chapter is my contribution to this process of professional empowerment for teachers who are responsible for the delivery of National Curriculum English. I address two issues: how we might seek out ways to engage with the complexities of teaching and learning English in order to reclaim control over the curriculum; and the scope of choices available as we interpret the statutory order. I shall propose that children's full access to language in school will be described, in part, by how those of us with professional expertise commit ourselves to exploring the opportunities both within and beyond the legal requirements.

What follows, therefore, is my analysis of the various curriculum documents in order to discover the assumptions they make about the development and functions of language, the opportunities still possible in the components which describe English and the restrictions which could limit children's full access to language in school.

I have organized the chapter around the four language modes that are set out in the National Curriculum: speaking, listening, reading and writing. However, in order to reduce the inevitable repetition in an analysis of interrelated areas, I have dealt somewhat arbitrarily with questions as they arise. To accommodate readers who are unfamiliar with the context in which the Statutory Order for English was created, I begin with the terms of reference.

Terms of reference
The proposals which gave rise to the National Curriculum for English can be found in the document *English for Ages 5 to 16* (DES, 1989). This is more usually referred to as 'The Cox Report'.

The terms of reference given to the Working Group for English by the former Secretary of State, Kenneth Baker, were explicit: English was to include language and literature and refer to media study and information technology. More specifically, it was required that care should be taken to provide close detail with regard to the nature, forms and functions of standard English, and also to ensure that all pupils have 'proper exposure to our great literary heritage' (DES, 1989, 2:3). These particular terms of reference, together with the demand that the proposals for English should be mapped out within the ten levels of the TGAT framework for assessment, have earned severe criticism from the teaching profession.

Keeping to these terms of reference, the Cox committee detailed the competence that all children in England and Wales should attain in three profile components: speaking and listening, reading, and writing. For primary children, learning English has two Key Stages for ages 5 to 7 and 7 to 11. These stages have within them ten Levels of Attainment, each describing what children should be able to do in order to reach the Attainment Targets which have been set. The levels are linked to the Programmes of Study which form the basis of what will be tested at ages 7 and 11 and what teachers are to teach. However, although a minimum content is prescribed, there is no legal requirement to restrict the curriculum to particular levels so the offer of a broad curriculum would still seem possible. Whether or not all children will be in a position to take it up, however, is the point at issue.

Before we turn to examine this challenge more closely, I want to draw attention to specific objectives that are set out for all children to learn.

There are just five Attainment Targets. For speaking and listening, children are to develop: 'Understanding of the spoken word and the capacity to express themselves effectively in a variety of speaking and listening activies, matching style and response to audience and purpose.' To meet the standards of attainment from Level 7, Key Stage 4, children should be using standard English whenever appropriate. In reading, the target is: 'The development of the ability to reach, understand and respond to all types of writing together with the development of information-retrieval strategies for the purposes of study.' For writing, children are to develop: 'A growing ability to construct and convey meaning in written language, matching style to audience and purpose.' There are also targets for spelling and handwriting in the primary school years.

Therefore, whatever is thought about the apparent familiarity of much of the Statutory Order for English, the stark reality is that there is a significant change in emphasis. Never before has so much political power been exerted over what children are to learn and how their progress is to be assessed and monitored throughout the primary school years and beyond.

In the next section we can consider the extent to which the writers of the Cox Report met the demands of a politically conservative Government and incorporated current and successful practices developed by teachers over the last two decades.

Towards an enlightened view of language

Earlier I suggested that many teachers would consider the Cox Report as offering an enlightened view about language. This is evidenced by: the emphasis placed on whole school policies for language; the interrelatedness of language modes; children learning language by using it both through interaction with each other and with texts; the significance given to talk in and beyond the classroom and on children's existing experience of writing as a starting point for development. Also, a broad range of literature which reflects a multicultural society is to be available and poetry, drama and media study are now an explicit part of all children's entitlement to language development in school. Furthermore, much of the advice given by the Cox committee on assessment by teachers is in keeping with the practice successfully developed since the Bullock Report (DES, 1975).

Teachers have given a cautious respect to the rational approach the report writers have taken in dealing with issues about language created by the specific terms of reference to standard English. The model of English which the Cox committee adopted was, in fact, the one worked out in the Kingman Report (DES, 1988). Thus they endorsed the view that:

> ...it is a clear responsibility of the English curriculum to extend children's use of varieties of language, to develop their capacity to understand written and spoken standard English and to teach them to write in conventional standard English. *(DES, 1989)*

Teachers have welcomed the acknowledgement that was given to the particular understanding of the differences which exist between schools in terms of linguistic backgrounds (DES, 1989, 4:6). Likewise they have welcomed the principle that because the language and culture of children's homes have a critical place in the classroom the curriculum should reflect the multicultural nature of British society. The writers of the Cox Report expressed particular concern for bilingual children: 'bilingual children should be considered an advantage in the classroom rather than a problem' (DES, 1989, 10:12). Moreover attention is drawn to the fact that bilingual and biliterate children may know more about language than their teachers (DES, 1989, 6:11).

Yet for all its apparent reasonableness and endorsement of one of the most cherished principles in primary education, that of starting with the children's existing language experience, there is a strong sense of unease among educators. This is because the National Curriculum for

English does not deal adequately with the actuality of linguistic diversity in British society and many of its schools.

Linking language so explicitly to a standard English for assessment and results betrays the apparent indifference of many legislators to the likely effect it may have on children whose relationship to the standard language of school has to be learnt. This is the crux of the problem which militates against the National Curriculum for English becoming a staging point for all children learning and developing language in an increasingly multicultural society. The issue is clear. The mandatory imposition of a model of standard English, and description of what it is all children should know about language at particular stages, is an ideological act. Children and parents need to know what is required for successful results in English from the outset of schooling alongside whatever else schools may offer for language development. According to the writers of the Cox Report, standard English is the dialect which has world-wide use, albeit with historical, geographical and social variations. They advise that it should be viewed both as a special kind of dialect rather than as just one amongst many and 'a social dialect, which happens to be the native language of certain social groups' (DES, 1989, 4:11). We could put this another way, as Margaret Meek (1991) has demonstrated, and say that the powerful users of standard English are those whose 'native' language is officially recognized as the critical one. The problem with which teachers have to deal, therefore, is not whether all children should learn standard English, for it is required by law and also for access to critical discourses in the wider community, rather the challenge is to ensure that children learn what they need to know about standard English, at the same time as developing a critical understanding of the nature and use of standard English.

Open debate about the ways in which schools contribute to the production and reproduction of class-related inequalities in the use of spoken and written language has never been easy to establish. Yet parents of working-class and bilingual children are well aware that full access to language in school is more complex and more difficult for their children than their middle-class peers. It seems that now is the time for long overdue open debate about this language issue.

Certainly the close monitoring and assessment of standard English heightens both the political and educational implications in teaching. If we accept that to be educated in our society means being confident and comfortable in using the culture's dominant linguistic resources, then all children should be aware of the power of those resources. Crucially, this means that all children are able to use a full range of linguistic repertoires, including being able to realize the power afforded them for their own chosen purposes. Research continues into the practices in many schools which have helped us to appreciate the close link between different social practices and different kinds of literacy. We now know more about the strong influence of early experience of language upon the different ways in which children use and learn language in school (Brice Heath, 1983; Levine, 1986; Street, 1984).

The ways in which future generations of children may come to use the standard English used in mainstream culture will therefore depend to some extent on how teachers and children view what counts as appropriate classroom discourse within the context of the National Curriculum. In the next section I begin this process of rationalization by examining the scope provided within the three components of the Statutory Order for exploring a full range of linguistic resources.

Speaking and listening

Traditionally oral language has not been perceived as having equal status with reading and writing in primary classrooms. Despite the seminal work by teachers in the 1970s (Britton, 1970; Barnes, 1976) and the official endorsement given to the value of talk in classrooms by the Bullock Report (DES, 1975), the importance of talk in learning has not been well developed within a coherently planned curriculum in all primary schools. Moreover collaborative learning and children's engagement in debate and well reasoned argument have not been much in evidence, either in research (Galton et al, 1980) or in reports by Her Majesty's Inspectorate (DES, 1978; DES, 1985; DES, 1990).

The Statutory Order for English, however, makes it plain that the silent classroom is no longer to be prized. Throughout the Programmes of Study, children are required to participate in groups as active speakers and listeners. References abound to their being able to 'hear books read'; 'take part'; 're-tell'; 'dramatize'; 'talk to the teacher'; 'say why'; 'ask and answer questions'; 'talk about'; 'discuss'; 'co-operate' and 'negotiate'. Interestingly, there is an emphasis on children learning in co-operative situations. At a time when so much stress is given to competition and differentiation, the opportunity for children to explore fully the direction which group co-operation may lead should not be overlooked by teachers. Certainly the importance of learning through interaction and alongside others has been well theorized (Vygotsky, 1978) and notable research leads us to recognize that there is a particular significance in the collaborative nature of learning at every stage of language development (Wells, 1985).

Another aspect in the Programmes of Study for speaking and listening which is particularly welcome are the opportunities for children to engage in imaginative work, role-play and improvised drama. Experienced teachers will be aware of the ways in which drama serves as an excellent medium for helping children to explore and reflect on their behaviour, and experience using language in order to make their knowledge explicit. Work by Halliday (1978) has helped us to recognize how young children use a wide range of registers in the context of certain speech events. Likewise we know that from a very early age children monitor and correct their own and others' linguistic performance (Oksaar, 1981). In this respect, therefore, one is able to see how it is possible for all children to talk about variations in vocabulary between different regional or social groups and for them to talk about some of the factors that influence people's attitudes to the way other people speak.

Unfortunately, whether this awareness of language is actually made explicit for all children depends on how constrained teachers are by the Levels of Attainment. For it is not until Level 5 in Key Stage 2 that children are expected to consider differences in vocabulary between regions and social groups and only children performing at Level 10 are expected to explore attitudes to spoken language and stereotyping.

A full commitment to implementing the Statutory Order would mean that opportunities are created for all children, from the outset of schooling, to engage in speaking and listening activities which help them explore their language productively within a wide range of contexts. The challenge teachers face is therefore in seeking out opportunities that extend and enrich children's experience of spoken language so that their implicit knowledge can be transformed into a more developed awareness.

By contrast a minimal commitment to developing children's speaking and listening competencies will mean restricting children to those attainment targets which have been prescribed for them. In the early years of schooling children are not required to develop their implicit knowledge of language, or take part in presentations, or solve problems through working with others, or offer opinions or state their personal feelings about an issue. This means that if a teacher were to deliver only the statutory minimum, most children in primary school would experience a less than adequate curriculum for developing their spoken language. Below Level 5 the main emphasis is on functional skills.

Children at Level 1, for instance, are expected to respond appropriately to simple instructions given by a teacher and then develop this ability so that by Level 3 they can 'give, receive and follow precise instructions'. Clearly such low expectations fail to acknowledge the experience of spoken language that young children bring to school. Moreover it fails to acknowledge the critical importance to all children, from the outset of schooling, of developing their knowledge of language, what its social functions are and how meanings are constructed in different contexts and by different groups.

It comes to this. Priority given to the development of spoken language, and thus the future we wish to nurture and make possible for all children to achieve in school, depends on how the curriculum is interpreted. Most children come to school confident and well disposed to use spoken language learned in the wider community. To go beyond the legal minimum provision for speaking and listening in school is to open up possibilities for developing what most children are able to do well. It is also for them to use and understand what they know about language and culture from their learning in different social contexts.

Unfortunately schools which require support in finding constructive ways of helping children engage with their knowledge about spoken language have not been assisted by the suppression of the Language in the National Curriculum (LINC) training materials. Given the enormous demands which primary teachers have to meet in delivering the whole curriculum, it would be understandable if they were to delay in engaging with more than is required of them. If this happens, it means that not all children will be given an opportunity to demonstrate what they can do or be given credit for it.

Writing

There has been much innovative practice and pioneering research concerned with children's writing development in recent years. The National Writing Project has supported the work of teachers engaged in finding ways of describing and evaluating the early stages of writing development and many accounts of classroom practices have been disseminated in consequent publications (Nelson, 1990). These practices are linked by two fundamental understandings: children in literate societies come to school with a knowledge of print (Clay, 1975; Ferreiro and Teberosky, 1979; Hall, 1989); and they have an awareness of how writing development helps to structure thinking. As a result of this kind of work more is known about the recursive ways in which much of children's writing develops. Children may experience early success in recognizing that print carries meaning and then appear to regress as they try out different ways of giving symbolic expression to this meaning. We do, however, have available sophisticated and effective ways of assessing this development, such as those described in the *Primary Language Record* (CLPE, 1988) and *Primary Learning Record* (CLPE, 1990).

The writers of the Cox Report were therefore prudent in paying close attention to current successful practices in their philosophy statements about writing. For instance, teachers are expected to write alongside and discuss writing with children. They are expected to adopt a variety of roles beyond, it seems, mere instructors in mechanical skills. This includes being 'observers, facilitators, modellers, readers and supporters' (DES 1989, 17:13). Significantly, particular emphasis is to be given to children's experience of the four interrelated language modes being developed in interactive contexts. Children are expected to write individually and in groups; share their personal writing with others; discuss what they have written and produce finished work for wider audiences. They are to know when and how to plan, draft, redraft, revise and proof read their work; and in the early stages of writing play is to be encouraged and respected. These are all positive and enlightened assumptions about the early stages of writing, and the role of the teacher, to which recent research will lend support.

The problem is that there is a profound contradiction between these assumptions and the linear, step by step and hierarchical way in which the Programmes of Study and Statements of Attainment describe language. The National Curriculum requires that all children's writing development is mapped out incrementally across levels which have been constructed for this purpose. Clearly, since much writing development is recursive, such linear Levels of Attainment can be, at best, only an approximate guide.

What then is the scope for teachers in their interpretation of the Statutory Order for English? Again, as was outlined in the earlier discussion about spoken language, the opportunities provided can be extended by transcending the linear structure which describes the Programmes of Study. There is no reason why, for example, many of the items set out in the Programmes of Study for children working towards Level 9 at Key Stage 4 could not equally be applied to earlier levels. Experienced primary school teachers know that many young children are capable of writing for unknown audiences by producing instructions for a game. They can also formulate hypotheses in writing and write about demanding subject matter. Many young children are able to redraft, revise and discuss writing and they are capable of writing in a variety of forms and for a range of purposes. Yet, if all children were to be restricted to the Programmes of Study which correspond to Levels of Attainment, only those who are classified as being between Levels 3 and 5 would be encouraged in these aspects of writing.

Thus, one of the challenges facing teachers wishing to offer more than the legal minimum required in the writing component is to find ways of transcending the levels that confine children's attainment. Another is the challenge in meeting the mandatory requirement that children are to be given systematic, sequential instruction at particular times. Irrespective of whatever else children may be attempting and succeeding with in their writing, they:

> ...should be taught how to spell words which occur frequently in their writing, or which are important to them, and those which exemplify regular spelling patterns. (DES, 1989, 17:39)

This implies a particular pedagogic stance and a view of learning which fails to give credit to children's ability to hypothesize and to their integrity as writers. Teachers know through experience, and research confirms, that the critical competencies required for fluency and correctness come from having a legitimate subject and a real audience rather than through instruction without a context (Bissex, 1980). In spelling, for instance, children move on from their own invented spellings to more conventional orthography through a process of intellectual search and concentrated effort which they associate with their own power to communicate.

Successful practices are those which support children in constructing and shaping the meanings they want to convey in writing. This is different from the idea that the development of conventional spelling and writing simply occurs by osmosis from childrens' interaction with texts and other people. We know that children require more than being bathed in language if they are to learn what it is critical for them to know about writing. On the other hand, it is also different from the idea that children require formal instruction and mechanical practice in mechanical skills if they are to learn conventional forms in written language. Children who are inexperienced with the conventional forms of standard English remain powerless as writers when pedagogies fail to help them see the significance of what their writing can do for them. Similarly failure to understand communication in terms of young children being able to use language to communicate power from the outset of formal schooling is to undermine notions of development.

It seems then that teachers who wish to make it possible for all children, working at all levels, to take up a full range of opportunities in their development as writers will have to find ways of accommodating legal requirements within a more informed and educationally pedagogic framework which lets children know what they have to be able to demonstrate in written language. They will also need to find ways of giving credit to those aspects of writing development which are not described within the Attainment Targets, especially at the lower levels. Parents will need information about the repeated trials children make to convey meaning; they will need to be aware of the significance of children's inventiveness and hypothesizing, and the value that authentic, committed and personal writing has throughout schooling.

Schools which already have well established ways of assessing and recording children's early writing development and have involved parents with this kind of information will be less problematic. The *Primary Language Record* and the *Primary Learning Record*, referred to earlier, are examples of ways of lending support to schools anxious to provide an accurate and humane account of children's writing development as well as satisfying the legal minimum requirement for reporting to parents.

On the other hand, teachers may wish to take an easier option which is to maintain that children will learn to write only because of and only what is explicitly taught in school. This would mean reducing children's writing competencies to those conventions and skills which have been duly prescribed within the Statutory Order.

Reading

All too often in the past, debate about reading in primary education has focused on the choice of materials and methods by which children may be taught to read. More recently, however, there has been much more attention paid to ways in which literacy is related to the lives, language, knowledge and experience of the children we teach. Increasingly, research has confirmed what many experienced teachers know about the value of the learning which children bring to the classroom. This has led to a re-examination and refinement of some practices which no longer seem appropriate for children growing up in a modern technological and multicultural society.

We know, for instance, that there is a powerful relationship between children's early experience of oral stories and literature in the development of literacy (Wells, 1986; Fox, 1983). We know that many children in literate communities have knowledge about print used in the environment (Hall, 1989) and that many children come to school with a highly sophisticated understanding of reading visual texts used in the media, especially television (Buckingham, 1990). Early success in reading is vitally important to children's later acquisition of literacy. Children who come to school with an extant wide understanding of texts are able to hypothesize and test out new words they come across both by trusting that the text will make sense and by practising what they already know (Meek, 1985, 1988, 1991; Smith, 1978).

This is not the same as saying that all children need is to be surrounded by books in order to become readers. On the contrary, it is a conception of reading as a learning and meaning-making experience. This idea has been duly endorsed by the Statutory Order for English in the National Curriculum documents. Recognition is given to the importance of children's early experience of language gained in the wider community and to reading activities which build on oral language. Children are also to experience a wide range of literature in school.

These are practices which are well established in many primary classrooms. Successful teachers also know that more is required than children developing and maintaining their enjoyment of literature if we want them to be able to participate fully in a democratic society. The final Attainment Target for reading makes this understanding explicit: all children are expected to understand and respond to all types of writing as well as develop information-retrieval strategies for the purposes of study. What we should not overlook here is the official recognition given to the importance of all children developing understanding of how texts are constructed through their early and continued engagement with literature. Moreover it is recognized that curriculum time should be set aside for personal reading. Interestingly enough, the use of reading schemes is neither endorsed nor encouraged.

The real challenge confronting all teachers, therefore, is not, in fact, how to raise scores on reading tests or select and grade reading materials, as certain aspects of the media and some uninformed politicians would have us believe. Rather, it is how to ensure that all children will be able to take advantage of the opportunities provided by a wide range of literature at whatever level of schooling. This is a challenge which exceeds by far the importance of the debates about whether or not standards are falling and methods of teaching which tend to force teachers into defensive positions.

A full commitment to the reading component will mean that all children are given opportunities to reflect on their personal response to texts and are able to engage purposefully with the demands different genres make on them as readers. Children working at all levels are to be helped to understand the nature of appositeness in context by reflecting upon what they recognize in the particularity of words used to effect a response. The communication of abstract ideas in a science investigation, for instance, may require specific vocabulary and forms of writing whereas a poem may require attention to words that elicit a more emotional response.

This does not necessarily mean that development in the ability to meet the demands of reading different kinds of literature and forming a response has to be confined to the subject English. Clearly, this is not the case. Primary school teachers are used to working with language across the curriculum and many will wish to continue to use this approach to exploit opportunities for language. Thus a child who has observed crystal formations in a science investigation or has discovered aesthetic qualities in a number pattern may choose to give them expression and shape in a poem or prose. However, now that the primary curriculum is officially described and assessed in subjects, there is a danger that the opportunities for learning in cross-curricular contexts will be less readily exploited. It will be important, therefore, that teachers continue to give attention to the affective and cognitive aspects in the National Curriculum for English. Otherwise, children's often early discovery of the differences between prose and verse may not be extended or developed fully.

Certainly, the argument that poetry, prose fiction and plays make powerful contributions both to personal and social learning, and to literacy development, is well established (Meek, 1988, 1991). Yet, it is often difficult for teachers to trust this view in practice by allocating the curriculum time and attention for children's personal reading. Now, with all the new demands created by the National Curriculum and the assessment procedures, some teachers may decide to compromise even more on the time required for children to share their ideas and responses that have been generated by their engagement with a wide experience of literature. Moreover, schools which do not already have a well-developed policy may find difficulty in making informed choices about the provision of a broad range of literature throughout the primary age range. Reports by Her Majesty's Inspectorate (DES, 1990) show that many primary schools do not have a coherent policy for literature. In this respect, the failure of the Cox Report to elucidate ways in which literature of all kinds may be made more accessible to children was of no help to many primary school teachers who are not specialists in the study of literature. They may, in principle, welcome the concept of literature as actively open to all children, such as evidenced in the philosophy statements in the report:

> Children should know about the processes by which meanings are conveyed and about the ways in which print carries values. *(DES, 1989, 2:23)*

However, without any clear guidance and in-service support as to how the development of a critical understanding relates to children's so-called personal response, this concept of literature may amount to little more than a pious notion that enjoyment of it makes us better people. After all, many primary teachers will not consider themselves specialists in literature and will not necessarily be familiar with accounts which explain the ways in which meanings and the development of a personal response are socially constructed (Foucault, 1980; Eagleton, 1983). Likewise, many teachers may not be used to talking about their response to texts or may not even read widely themselves.

Drama and media studies are two of the ways in which children's active engagement with texts and ability to act upon the world may be developed effectively. Sadly, both are seriously underplayed within the statutory curriculum. For this reason I would argue that the links between literary texts, drama and the media, warranted a more explicit place in the Statements of Attainment for reading. Instead, drama appears only in the Programmes of Study and media study is linked only to non-literary texts. The use of information technology, moreover, in rewriting and representing texts of all kinds, is not mentioned.

There are also serious financial constraints which may militate against teachers being able to make a full commitment to the Statutory Order for English. Many schools struggling to provide a wide range of good quality books for their children know of the almost prohibitive expense which is incurred. And, it is precisely those schools, in poor areas, where children have most to gain from a wide provision of literature, which are most likely to find difficulty. The sad paradox is that schools which can rely on income from fund raising to supplement insufficient resources are likely to serve communities where good quality books are luxuries that are afforded by many homes.

It would hardly be surprising then, given the lack of sustained in-service support and adequate funding, if some teachers opted for a minimal commitment to interpreting the demands made by the Statutory Order for English. They may prefer to look more towards how it fits in with their existing policies rather than be prepared to question and open up debate about how school practices are related to children becoming readers and being able to engage with literature critically. Interestingly enough the results of the National Curriculum Council's (NCC, 1991) evaluation of the first year of the new curriculum reveal that less time is being given to children's personal reading due to curriculum demands made in science and mathematics. Literature-based topic work is becoming increasingly rare as teachers are, apparently, finding they can more easily accommodate the Statutory Order for English during a science topic than deliver the science content through literature. Given the critical importance of reading it remains to be seen what long-term effects these kind of compromises will have on children becoming readers.

Conclusion

Any curriculum for English, mandatory or otherwise, will not by itself guarantee that all children's language is enriched and extended. Neither will it ensure that their literacy is used powerfully. It will not remove inequalities and it will not transform children's experience of power-lessness and difference. What it can do is provide a structure and content which appeals to the imagination and intellect of children and teachers in a way that invites them to question, to challenge and to conceive of alternatives.

My analysis of the National Curriculum for English leads me to the conclusion that teachers will need to make a significant leap in imagination to transcend and transform the rigid terms in which it is described. Above all, it will require that they recognize their power in interpreting the Statutory Order through their relationships with children, parents and the wider community. Otherwise, evidence of the kind of learning which is still possible but is not set out within the Levels of Attainment will count for little.

What we should not overlook, however, is the fact that for the first time in primary education we have a common point of reference and a national forum for critical debate. A useful place to begin using this opportunity will be to engage in informed and open debate about issues identified within this chapter. After all, the children in our schools today will not have another chance to experience the critical primary years of education. Becoming fluent and confident in English, upon which so much other learning depends, remains a challenge. It is this challenge which no one concerned with education can afford to ignore.

References

Barnes, D. (1976) *From Communication to Curriculum*. Penguin.

Bennet, J. (1982) *Learning to Read with Picture Books*. Signal Press

Bissex, G. (1980) *Gnys at Wrk*. Harvard University Press.

Buckingham, D. (1990) *Watching Media Learning; Making Sense of Media Education*. Lewes: Falmer Press.

Brice Heath, S. (1983) *Ways with Words*. Cambridge: Cambridge University Press.

Britton, J. (1970) *Language and Learning*. Pelican.

CLPE (Centre for Language in Primary Education) (1988) *Primary Language Record Handbook*. London: CLPE.

CLPE (Centre for Language in Primary Education) (1990) *Patterns of Learning, Primary Learning Record and the National Curriculum*. London: CLPE.

Clay, M. (1975) *What Did I Write?: Beginning Writing Behaviour*. Heinemann.

Department of Education and Science (1975) *A Language for Life*. HMSO.

Department of Education and Science (1978) *Primary Education in England*. HMSO.

Department of Education and Science (1985) *Better Schools*. HMSO.

Department of Education and Science (1988) *Report of the Committee of Inquiry into the Teaching of English Language*. London: HMSO.

Department of Education and Science (1989) *English for Ages 5 to 16*. (The Cox Report.) HMSO.

Department of Education and Science (1990) *Aspects of Primary Education: The Teaching and Learning of Language and Literacy*. HMSO.

Eagleton, T. (1983) *Criticism and Ideology*. Oxford: Blackwell.

Ferreiro, E. and Teberosky, A. (1979) *Literacy Before Schooling*. Heinemann.

Foucault, M. (1980) *Paver/Knowledge: Selected Interviews and Other Writings 1972–1977*.

Fox, C. (1983) 'Floppies will make them Grunt.' In: *Opening Moves: Bedford Way Papers*.

Friere, P. (1972) *Pedagogy of the Oppressed*. Penguin.

Galton, M., Simon, B. and Croll (1980) *Inside the Primary Classroom*. London: Routledge & Kegan Paul.

Hall, N. (1989) In: Hall, N. (ed.) *The Emergence of Authorship in Young Children*. Hodder & Stoughton.

Halliday, M. A. K. (1978) *Language as a Social Semistic*. Arnold.

Levine, J. (1986) *The Social Context of Literacy*. Routledge.

Meek, M. (1985) *Learning to Read*. Bodley Head.

Meek, M. (1988) *How Texts Teach What Readers Learn*. Thimble Press.

Meek, M. (1991) *On Becoming Literate*. Bodley Head.

National Curriculum Council (1991) *Report on Monitoring the Implementation of National Curriculum Core Subjects 1989–90*. York: NCC.

Nelson (1990) *Writing and Learning*. Netson.

Oksaar, E. (1981) 'Linguistic and pragmatic awareness of monolingual and multilingual children.' In: Dale, P. and Ingram, D. (eds) *Child Language: An International Perspective*. Baltimore: University Park Press.

SCDC (1987-1991) *The National Oracy Project*. SCDC.

Smith, F. (1978) *Reading*. Heinemann.

Street, B. (1984) *Literacy in Theory and Practice*. Cambridge: Cambridge University Press.

Vygotsky, L. (1978) *Mind in Society*. Cambridge, Massachusetts: MIT Press.

Walkerdine, V. (1980) *Democracy in the Kitchen*. Virago.

Wells, G. (1985) *Language and Learning: An Interactional Perspective*. Falmer.

Wells, G. (1986) In: *The Meaning Makers*. Hodder & Stoughton, 1987.

Chapter Two
Mathematics: Rhetoric and Practice in Primary Teaching

Andrew Brown

Introduction

There is no shortage of statements about what primary school teachers should be doing to be effective teachers of mathematics. We are told, for instance, that we should work in an open and exploratory way, make good use of practical activity, encourage collaborative work, develop problem-solving skills, foster confidence in using mathematics, provide meaningful contexts for mathematical activities, facilitate discussion of mathematical ideas, build on children's existing strategies, avoid over-reliance on schemes, and so on. Those of us with a particular interest in the teaching and learning of mathematics may feel broad agreement with what is being encouraged here. We might be concerned, however, that there appears to be little evidence of many of these practices in the classroom (DES/HMI, 1989; Desforges and Cockburn, 1987). It thus seems to be relatively easy to debate and define what 'good practice' in the teaching and learning of primary mathematics might be, but somewhat more difficult to translate this into classroom practice. We might also ask, in the light of this, how a set of principles and associated practices come to appear to have some form of unity and coherence, and how it is that this can be recognized as constituting 'good practice' by most primary teachers.

The National Curriculum for mathematics has, of course, provoked a further deluge of statements regarding 'good practice', together with initiatives that attempt to lay the foundations for the development of such practices in schools. I do not wish this article to make a further contribution to this rapidly expanding universe of statements, nor do I want to attempt to tell the Government how the sets of statements that constitute the National Curriculum might be turned into sets of actual classroom practices. Rather I want to look critically at the relationship between 'what is said about teaching mathematics' and 'what teachers do'. This involves examining the kinds of statements that are made about primary mathematics teaching, which in turn leads to looking more closely at the notion of 'good practice' itself. The effects of defining particular ways of working as being 'good practice' will be considered, and doubts raised about the very notion that there can some form of direct translation of rhetoric into practice as is often presumed. On the basis of this discussion I wish then tentatively to offer some suggestions as to how we might conceptualize the relationship between statements about practice and development of practice in school, and how we as practitioners might constructively orientate ourselves towards these statements in the development of our own practice.

Implicit in this is the view that mathematics is in a distinctly different position to other elements of the primary curriculum. There continues to be a widespread anxiety about the teaching of mathematics both amongst teachers and beyond the school. For this reason it is all the more important to avoid falling into the position of stating yet again what 'good practice' is, or declaring that the National Curriculum will enable 'good practice' to continue. We need, rather, to consider carefully how change in the teaching of mathematics in the primary school might be facilitated, which in turn may lead us to question the types of strategies that have been adopted in attempting to develop mathematics teaching in the classroom.

Mathematics in the National Curriculum

Already the mathematics component of the National Curriculum and the continuing debates surrounding it seem to have been with us for an awfully long time. A Working Group was set up in July 1987 with the brief to advise the Government on appropriate Attainment Targets and Programmes of Study for mathematics. The passage between this point and the production of the final Statutory Orders, laid before Parliament in March 1989, was by no means easy. The tensions and difficulties manifest in this process are in many respects still current and are thus worthy of brief consideration.

A degree of conflict between the expectations of the Secretary of State for Education and what we might call the 'mathematics education community' was obvious from the very start and perhaps came to a head publicly on the publication of the Interim Report in December 1987. This was not favourably received by the Secretary of State (DES and WO, 1988, pp. 99–101), although many of the statements made did appear to have the support of mathematics educators (ibid, pp. 102–103). This signals a central problem. The terms of reference for the Working Group stressed that it should take account of 'best practice and the results of relevant research and curriculum developments' (ibid, p. 92). This is reinforced in the Secretary of State's letter to the Chair of the Working Group giving more detailed guidance on the task of the Group (ibid, pp. 93–98). Here it is stated that the Group should draw on the earlier reports as a starting point and that it might look to 'good practice in those LEAs that have developed effective and well-founded policies for mathematics' and 'the collective wisdom and experience of the professional bodies such as the Association of Teachers of Mathematics and the Mathematical Association' (ibid, p. 97). It becomes inevitable that key features of the rhetoric of mathematics education are going to conflict both with the very nature of the task of producing a hierarchy and the views of those people who do not form part of the professional community who produce this rhetoric.

The notion that mathematics can be organized hierarchically for the purposes of teaching and learning is an obvious point of tension. The Secretary of State expressed that he was 'disappointed' in the Working Group's failure to make progress in this area in his response to the Interim Report. Within mathematics education, however, the extent to which such a hierarchy can be formed is a matter of considerable debate (see Noss, Goldstein and Hoyles, 1989; O'Reilly, 1990; Küchemann, 1990). Tensions were also manifest in the Secretary of State's reflections on the use of calculators: 'your final report will need to recognize the risks as well as the opportunities which calculators in the classroom offer' (DES and WO, 1988, p. 100). Related areas of conflict include the place of 'more traditional pencil and paper practice of important skills and techniques' and 'basic numerical competence' (ibid, p. 100). Such conflicts were to manifest themselves again in the debate over the third profile component, dealing specifically with 'practical applications of mathematics', proposed by the Working Group in its formal proposals published in August 1988. It was proposed that this profile component, consisting of three Attainment Targets (using mathematics, communication skills, and personal qualities), be given a 40 per cent weighting at each Key Stage. Despite gaining overwhelming support for its retention through the consultation exercise, this profile component was removed from the final report, as suggested by the Secretary of State, and replaced by two Attainment Targets, one in each of the remaining two profile components (see Noss, 1990, for a discussion of this).

It is unnecessary to dwell too long on aspects of the genealogy of mathematics in the National Curriculum. Some reflection on this is, however, important. To an extent, everything we now do or say about the teaching and learning of primary mathematics bears the traces of the National Curriculum. It is vital, therefore, that we take care not to allow the structure, orientation and content of the Statutory Orders to submerge to such an extent that they become invisible, lodging themselves in the depths of our consciousness as necessary and uncontested parts of the foundations of 'good practice' itself. Whilst the call to 'roll up our sleeves and get on with it' (Margaret Brown, 1989) might be understandable, this does tend to make such critical consideration seem obstructive. We have to be aware of what it is that gave rise to both the form and the content of the Statutory Orders, of what is included, what is not, and why this is so. This diverts us from the temptation to attribute any essential value to the particularities of the orders and from the desire to look for definitive meanings for the Statements of Attainment and a unity and coherence in their presentation. It also helps us in a particular reading of the Non-Statutory Guidance (NSG) produced in June 1989. The NSG for mathematics states that:

> The purpose of these guidance materials is to help teachers in their task of interpreting and implementing National Curriculum mathematics as set out in the Statutory Orders for mathematics. *(para. 1.1)*

The guidance notes are widely perceived and celebrated, however, as reaffirmation of 'good practice' in the teaching of mathematics. They can be seen as providing a bridge between the rhetoric of mathematics education and the structure and content of the Statutory Orders. The NSG appears to fulfil the role of reinserting those elements of the rhetoric that have been squeezed out of the Statutory Orders or represented in them in an unacceptable way. Thus an attempt can be seen to be made to resolve some of the tensions and conflicts noted above. The most fundamental of these, namely, hierarchies, is dealt with in the following way:

> Although mathematics does contain a hierarchical element, learning in mathematics does not necessarily take place in completely predetermined sequences. Mathematics is a structure composed of a whole network of concepts and relationships, and, when being used, mathematics becomes a living process of creative activity. *(para. 2.6)*

This would seem much more in line with the critiques of the mathematics component of the National Curriculum produced by mathematics educators than with the Statutory Orders to which the NSG is appended. Much of what follows in the NSG can be read as an attempt to bring together, or overlay, the structures and contents of the Statutory Orders with the rhetoric of 'good practice' in the teaching and learning of mathematics. The notes also deal with, amongst other things, the relationship between mental calculations, pencil and paper methods and the use of calculators, and using and applying mathematics. These issues are familiar from the discussion above.

We thus have an attempt to pull together the Statutory Orders and forms of practice that are recognized by mathematics educators as acceptable. The Statements of Attainment and the associated assessment procedures thus have to be rendered compatible with 'good practice'. So, it appears as if 'good practice' might win out in the end. Is this something to celebrate, however? What is 'good practice' and what are its effects? How helpful is the notion of 'good practice' and how useful for teachers are statements made on the basis of presumed 'good practice'?

'Good practice' in the teaching of primary mathematics
Before we consider what, in England and Wales in the 1990s, might be considered 'good practice' in the teaching of mathematics in the primary school, it might be fruitful to consider how the term itself works. What is the significance of saying that something is an example, or constituent, of 'good practice'? This certainly implies that the person or persons identifying something as 'good practice' are in a position to make or relay some sort of valid judgement. It implies that the practice being invoked is in some sense professionally acceptable and that it is effective in some way. The basis on which these claims are made is rarely rendered explicit: how can its acceptability be established and how is the effectiveness of the practice evaluated? Often it is the 'authority' – in terms of 'standing' rather than structural terms – of those making the statements that establishes the former with the latter as a presumed correlate. The term 'good practice' thus gains its power by signalling a wide general professional acceptability that in turn implies some form of effectiveness. Let us take the oft quoted paragraph 243 of the Cockcroft Report (Cockcroft et al, 1982) as an example. It states:

> Mathematics teaching at all levels should include opportunities for: exposition by the teacher; discussion between teacher and pupils and between pupils themselves; appropriate practical work; consolidation and practice

of fundamental skills and routines; problem solving, including the application of mathematics to everyday situations; investigational work.

It would be no exaggeration to say that every primary teacher in England and Wales must be familiar with this list. The six items have, in effect, become central criteria for the evaluation of mathematical work and have left their mark on all aspects of initial and in-service training and become reference points for writing about the teaching and learning of mathematics. Where, however, do these items come from? How can they be so confidently stated as the foundations of good mathematical work? The paragraph continues:

> In setting out this list we are aware that we are not saying anything which has not already been said many times and over many years. The list that we have given has appeared, by implication if not explicitly, in official reports, DES publications, HMI discussion papers and the journals and publications of the professional mathematical associations. Yet we are aware that although there are classrooms in which the teaching includes, as a matter of course, all the elements we have listed, there are many in which the mathematics teaching does not include even a majority of these elements.

This paragraph neatly reveals the way in which 'good practice' does its work. Its constituents are validated on the basis that they have been circulated around the professional community: there is apparently no need to provide any evidence for their effectiveness. It also acts to define the practice of 'many' teachers in terms of 'lack': their (or is it our?) practice is not adequate in that it does not exhibit the elements of 'good practice' outlined. Thus the adequacy of classroom practices is judged not on the basis of whether or not they are effective, however this might be defined and judged, nor is it evaluated in relation to the particular circumstances in which children and teachers are working. Adequacy is judged, rather, on the basis of degree of match to a list of decontextualized ideal practices. There thus appears to be no problem in stating alongside this confidently articulated list that these practices have been advocated for some considerable time and that, despite this, they are not a widespread feature of observed classroom practice. In addition there appears to be no need to attempt to support the assertions made with any form of evidence. In fact the inscription of statements in such reports then goes on to constitute evidence in other contexts. For instance, Preston cites statements made in the Cockcroft report as 'evidence' (Preston, 1987, p .7), in this instance, of the existence of a poor match between mathematical content and chosen teaching methods. More recently specific statements about what constitutes 'good practice' in the teaching of primary mathematics have been made by HMI (DES/HMI, 1989). These statements are presented alongside a report on the state of the teaching of primary mathematics culled from general inspections carried out between 1982 and 1986. This report makes fairly depressing reading. It was obviously fairly depressing for the HMI too as, rather than construct the section on the characteristics of 'good practice' in primary mathematics from their observations of the 285 inspections carried out, they chose to visit a further 70 schools 'in which good practice in mathematics had been identified' (ibid, para. 37).

The features of 'good practice' elaborated come as no surprise. They include: fostering a positive attitude to mathematics; emphasis on the application of mathematics; well-planned work; children formulating, testing and revising hypotheses; work on pattern and relationships; a variety of approaches to calculation used; sensible use of the calculator; extensive experience of measurement and estimation; clear policies on mathematics; individual, group and whole class work as appropriate; opportunities for co-operative work; positive and well timed teacher intervention; meeting needs through the differentiation of work; use of practical and first-hand experience; cross-curricular work; appropriate reflection of cultural diversity; relevant exploratory work; stimulating working environment; effective teaching. This list obviously does not do full justice to the document, but it does give some flavour of the types of statements made and their consistency with those made in earlier publications.

The constituents of 'good practice' are drawn from a variety of contexts but are presented as a unity. This implies that 'good practice' has some kind of material existence separate from the conditions of its production: these are the practices that indicate that good mathematical work is going on. This has a number of effects. For one it creates a set of criteria for judging, on the level of what is apparent, the quality of work. Obviously the existence of what are in effect indicators is of particular use to groups like HMI who have to make judgements on the basis of such observations. It also fosters the belief that it is the universality of particular *practices* that should be encouraged, rather than the universality of particular *principles* or *outcomes*. In somewhat simple terms this means that it appears less important that we as teachers are founding our activity on shared sets of underlying principles or are judging what we do on the basis of whether there are particular similarities in outcomes or achievements than it is that we are all doing the same thing. Alternatively the argument might run that there is some kind of essential link between all three with the priority on practices – that is, that if we do the same things, principles and outcomes fall into line. Ascribing particular essential effects to practices hardly seems tenable (Brown, 1985, 1990).

This kind of attitude has been, it would be fair to say, a feature of primary schooling for some time. Hence practices, such as the mounting and display of children's work in a certain way, the use of particular forms of classroom organization, the utilization of specified procedures or pieces of equipment, and so on, become essential features of 'good primary practice' irrespective of the particular conditions teachers and children are working in. Teachers and schools, and even local authorities, come to be judged as being 'one of us' (ie good practitioners) on the basis of whether they exhibit these practices. This reaches its most problematic form when 'English primary practice' is exported and encouraged in countries with very different sets of social, cultural and economic circumstances. Somehow the 'quality' of education comes to be located in, for instance, the creation of particular types of wall displays of children's work that may, in certain circumstances, have a completely different cultural meaning and, in any case, not be economically viable.

Interestingly the statements made cover not only the characteristics of the school, the classroom and the practices of the teachers but also the characteristics of the teachers and the children themselves. For instance, in describing the schools where 'good practice' was identified, HMI say that 'it is significant that in these schools mathematics was perceived by teachers and pupils alike as a lively, dynamic and enjoyable subject' (DES/HMI, 1989, para. 39). Along with the other statements made, this acts to construct a decontextualized ideal practitioner, in relation to whom all other teachers are placed, either favourably or unfavourably (and not just in terms of practice, but also attitudes and orientations).

The above is not intended as a criticism of the HMI document, as it effectively achieves what it sets out to do [1]. It is, rather, a questioning of

---

1   Indeed an attempt is made to contextualize the given images of good practice by providing examples of actual activities observed. This is very effective in driving home the HMI view of what good practice is, but is obviously limited in terms of affecting the practice of those teachers who may not see themselves, for a variety of reasons, as being able to set up activities of a similar form.

the construction of, and effects of, the notion of 'good practice'. This creates a veneer of apparent usefulness and relevance, but how effective is this in terms of the transformation of practice? Do teachers really not demonstrate the characteristics of 'good practice' because they do not know what these characteristics are?

So far we have indulged in a discussion of solely 'what is said or written about the teaching and learning of primary mathematics', but this is not to say that the discussion is trivial. Notions of 'good practice' do have significant power. As pointed out above, 'what is said' acts to provide a framework and points of reference for the judgement both of observed practices and our own practice as teachers. This circulation of evaluation criteria actually pre-dates us as teachers. We enter teaching through this universe of statements about what it is to be a good teacher and our success as teachers is gauged in relation to these. We need also to ask what our experience, as teachers or as trainees, of 'good practice' is. Are our own images of 'good practice' drawn from our own direct experience and presence or are they drawn from reading, listening to the accounts of others or through other representations such as video? I do not wish to prioritize direct experience over other forms of experience here but, rather, I want to signal the importance of considering the origins and effects of 'what is said'. This involves treating these statements not merely as representations of 'good practice' but also in some sense as constitutive of orientations towards practice.

The relationship between rhetoric and practice

In terms of general primary practice there is an acknowledged history of disparity between 'what is said' and 'what is done' [2]. Simon (1981) has, for instance, documented the variance between the types of statements made about primary school practice in the Plowden Report (Central Advisory Council for Education (England), 1967), and later popularized in a number of other publications during the following decade, and evidence collected at the time regarding classroom practice. He demonstrates that there is little evidence that the 'revolution' in primary education that was widely thought to have occurred actually manifested itself to any substantial degree in classroom practices across the country.

---

2   This is not, of course, to suggest that such a separation is not also a feature of other phases of the schooling system.

A similar separation between rhetoric and practice seems to hold with the teaching of primary mathematics today.

The HMI document (DES/HMI, 1989) provides some evidence for this. On the basis of their initial 285 full inspections they report that, for instance:

> Arithmetic was given a lot of attention in all the schools ... In the vast majority of schools performance in computation was adequate and it was good in almost half the schools. Even so, in many cases, pupils were unable to apply the skills of computation reliably in practical situations. *(para. 7)*

Successive reports and surveys have revealed, and criticized, this concentration on arithmetic in primary mathematics. They have also stressed the importance of being able to apply arithmetic skills and concepts. There has also been consistent stress on the importance of finding a meaningful context for mathematical work and thus on developing mathematics within cross-curricular work. The observations of HMI indicate that, despite this, there has been little development at the level of the classroom.

> Though most schools established some cross-curricular links, bringing mathematics together with other subjects, on the whole this work was undeveloped and mathematics was practised as a discrete study. The proportion of schools achieving successful and sustained links between mathematics and other areas of the curriculum was about one in six. *(para. 15)*

Again, on the recurring issue of the over-reliance of teachers on published mathematics schemes, they report that:

> Only in the minority of classes did teachers use published materials selectively as part of a broader strategy of teaching, choosing suitable resources to match a programme of work to the needs and abilities of individual children. *(para. 17)*

Later in the document, in contrast to this, HMI state the orthodox position on 'good practice' with respect to mathematics schemes:

> There was little evidence to suggest that heavy reliance on routine sessions of mathematics based on textbooks and published workcards resulted in the most effective learning. On most occasions, where parallel classes worked in different ways, the mental agility, flexibility and capacity to respond

appropriately to mathematical challenges was markedly less good in those classes that were fed a constant diet of work based on commercial material. *(para. 74)*

This of course relates to the question of the organization of children for mathematical work and the Cockcroft Report's suggestion that a variety of forms of organization – individual work, group work and work with the whole class – should be used as appropriate. HMI observe that:

> In seeking to match the level of work to each pupils ability, teachers set individual assignments, in the main making use of textbooks and work-cards. This tended to be the predominant teaching strategy, with the result that there were too few occasions of direct teaching to the whole class or a particular group in order to consolidate the children's grasp of important mathematical principles and allow their findings and difficulties to be discussed. *(para. 19)*

This obviously also relates to paragraph 243 of the Cockcroft Report reproduced earlier. Despite the clarity with which the criteria for the organization of mathematical work were stated by Cockcroft and the extent to which these were disseminated and taken on as vital components of the rhetoric of mathematics education, they appear to have had relatively little impact on practice. This view is reinforced by the observation that, with reference to problem-solving, relevance and the opportunities provided by other areas of the curriculum:

> ...for the most part mathematics is still taught as a separate subject in relative isolation from the rest of the curriculum. Insufficient emphasis is given to extended problem-solving and the application of mathematics to daily life. In these matters the general picture remains much as it did in the 1970s. *(para. 28)*

In concluding this overview they state that:

> Many of the shortcomings identified in the 1978 survey characterise mathematical work in many primary schools today: too narrow a range of work with too much emphasis on repeated mechanical computation unassociated with day-to-day realities; insufficient opportunities for children to consolidate their mathematical skills by applying them to relevant problem-solving; not enough time devoted to effective discussion or exposition of mathematical ideas; children of high mathematical ability insufficiently challenged. *(para. 34)*

It would be stretching definitions a little to consider HMI inspections as research. There is, in fact, relatively little published research on the form of classroom practices in the teaching of primary mathematics in England and Wales. Two post-Cockcroft studies (Desforges and Cockburn, 1987; Stow, 1988) do, however, bear out some aspects of the observations made by HMI.

Desforges and Cockburn carried out a detailed study of the practice of seven experienced infant teachers who had expressed a particular interest in the teaching of mathematics. Amongst their findings they note teachers' 'relative lack of attention to inculcating the higher order skills of problem solving, applications work and open-ended exploration' (ibid, p. 123). They state, for instance, that:

> From our perspective the major, immediate impressions of classroom mathematics were a lot of extremely industrious children responding to efficient and business-like teachers and engaged, in the main, in exercises drawn from commercial schemes. Whilst practical work was evident, it played, by and large, only a supporting role to paper and pencil work. The children rarely tackled real problems in their mathematics or applied their thoughts to anything other than the procedures demanded by the worksheets. *(ibid, p. 79)*

Stow's study, carried out under the auspices of the National Foundation for Educational Research, focuses on the work of the mathematics co-ordinator, or post-holder, in the primary school. She suggests, on the basis of a large-scale survey and a smaller number of interviews, that little time is given over to such work and that as a result what is achieved is by and large fairly limited. HMI comments confirm this: whilst acknowledging that the proportion of schools that have a mathematics co-ordinator has increased (from just under a half in 1978 to two-thirds in 1986) they note that there are 'relatively few schools where the duties of the co-ordinator include the majority of those suggested in the Cockcroft Report' (DES/HMI, 1989, para. 30). Strangely, in the same paragraph, the idea that as many schools as possible should have such a member of staff is cited as an example of 'a number of practical suggestions' that the Cockcroft Report has to make for schools. It appears that practicality is judged on the ease with which a statement can be made, its acceptability in terms of prevalent rhetoric and its apparent relevance to practice rather than its feasibility and effectiveness. In describing the apparent effectiveness of the mathematics post-holder within the school, HMI noted that in only about one in four schools did the post-holder have a noticeable effect on the quality of the work in the school and that little time was available to the post-holder to provide the type of support sanctioned by the Cockcroft Report. Here we have, perhaps, an indication of one of the features of the relationship between rhetoric and practice.

The above indicates a significant gap between the rhetoric of primary mathematics, with its particular images of 'good practice', and actual classroom practices. This is not to suggest that 'good practice' as framed above does not exist in any tangible form, but rather that it is not widespread. It is thus not helpful to continue to assert that all is well as 'good practice' can continue in the era of the National Curriculum. 'Good practice' functions in a number of ways. It does not, however, act to describe common practice, nor does the continual restatement of the characteristics of 'good practice' appear to help to establish these practices. In the light of such assertions it might be tempting to pathologize teachers and ask, as do Desforges and Cockburn, why it is that primary teachers do not take the advice they are given on the teaching of mathematics. In contrast to this I wish to focus on those situations in which changes do take place and to suggest a reorientation of the relationship between rhetoric and practice. Fundamental to this is questioning the assumptions that if a practice can be stated and become an element of primary rhetoric then it is necessarily practically feasible, and that if a particular practice is observed in one context it is possible to reproduce it with similar effects in other contexts.

Change in the teaching of primary mathematics
Desforges and Cockburn suggest that:

> The major responsibility for desired changes lies with LEA officers, HMIs and theorists who should work to provide teachers with (i) an assessment context which unavoidably rates processes over products; (ii) intellectual tools and curriculum conceptions appropriate to the rhetoric of aspirations; and (iii) the time and circumstances in which to operate the desired techniques. *(Desforges and Cockburn, 1987, p. 156)*

This statement, whilst appearing to support classroom teachers by locating the responsibility for facilitating change elsewhere, embodies a central problem. A particular relationship between those agents that generate the rhetoric of primary mathematics education and the teacher is presumed[3]. The former are seen to provide the aims, tools and resources for the latter: the teacher thus comes to be seen as a technician, employing a range of available techniques to move towards already defined ends. Not only this but a high degree of control of the circumstances in which teachers work is also presumed. Elsewhere I have argued that such a view, a form of technical rationalism, is untenable (Brown, 1990) as there are contingencies that act to make the circumstances in one school, or classroom, possibly very different from another within the same administrative, policy and resourcing framework. One such contingency might be, for instance, the relationship between the implicit and explicit demands of the school and the culture and expectations of the children and their parents. An earlier study (Brown, 1985) has indicated that within the same local authority different forms of relations between a school and its intake can give rise to different patterns of change within the school.

The concern Desforges and Cockburn have for outcomes is certainly a step forward from the HMI concern with specific practices as the latter presumes a match between practices and outcomes which is independent of context. None the less it represents a particular positioning of the teacher. They call for theorists to 'come clean' about the difficulties of, for instance, teaching higher order thinking skills. Researchers and academics are implored to be more realistic. Whilst we might have some degree of sympathy with this, it does nothing to disturb the presumed hierarchy of the specialist, but generalizable, expertise of the researcher/academic and the general, but localized, competence of the teacher. It also neglects to consider the complexity of the relationship between theory, research and practice.

In order to address this it is necessary to consider briefly the conditions of production of academic knowledge and the relationship between what is produced and action in the field of primary schooling. Academic

---

3　Of course the teacher may be, through participation in the work of a professional association, through part-time research or through in-service training activities, as well as through everyday engagement in discussions about practice, one of those generating rhetoric. This signals the complexity of the issue and the particular attention that has to be paid to the question of identity. There is a multiplicity of dimensions to a teacher's identity and the relationship between different aspects of this is of great interest. The particular case of teachers, who are also parents, taking part in discussions about the participation of parents in schooling has been considered by Brown (in press).

work is produced in a specific context which acts to define what might be an important and/or interesting question, how one might go about addressing such a question, what constitutes valid and valuable work and so on. Such work is presented to an audience of peers in a particular way, for instance through academic papers and journal articles, and provokes certain types of responses. The work might appear to have 'implications for practice' in a context outside the academic world of its production, in which case a recontextualization (Bernstein, 1990) takes place. This involves the work, or more likely particular aspects of it, being lifted from the context in which it was produced, evaluated and disseminated, and placed into a different context in which different sets of concerns hold sway. The recontextualization of elements of the work of Jean Piaget and of Basil Bernstein provide examples of the most obvious effects of this (Walkerdine, 1984, 1988; Atkinson, 1985). In both cases work that was produced within particular academic fields, structural epistemology and socio-linguistics respectively, was perceived to speak directly to the classroom practitioner. The lifting of aspects of this work from their academic contexts and placement in the field of informing educational action gave rise to notions of 'readiness' in the case of Piaget's work and 'linguistic deficit' in Bernstein's. In both cases there certainly seems to be tension between these notions, as disseminated through, for instance, teacher training, and other aspects of their academic work. It is not being suggested here that there has been simply a misunderstanding of academic work but that the shift from one context to another lends different meanings to the statements made. The point is a complex one and this brief account does not do it justice. The crux of the argument is that there is no straightforward, unambiguous communication between the world of academic production and that of educational action. The conditions of production and validation of academic work and those of classroom practice are distinctly different. The former does not, and cannot, produce prescriptions or tools for the latter. This is not to say, however, that there is no relationship between these two fields. It is, rather, a recognition that it is the form of relationship that is under question.

The consequences of recontextualization are further compounded by the position of those who affect the recontextualization of statements. These are likely to include teacher trainers, college lecturers, local authority inspectors and advisers, INSET providers, members of professional associations and so on. The interests of, and pressures acting on, people working in this field are different from those of day-to-day classroom practice and hence the meanings given to what is said, and to what is utilized in saying these things, are likely to differ. It is important to note that it is the field of recontextualization that creates this effect, not particular individuals within it. Researchers and academics can, of course, recontextualize their own work (for instance Hughes, 1986, produces his own list of the implications of his research for the practice of teachers of primary mathematics) but this does not free them from the effects of recontextualization. Similarly classroom teachers, perhaps within the context of study for a higher degree, might also themselves effect a recontextualization of academic work. It is the moving between contexts, and thus the characteristics of the contexts, that largely structures the transformation, not the particular agents of this. It is obviously not just academic work that gets recontextualized in this way; 'experience' and other statements about practice get the same treatment, for instance, in being invoked as the basis for statements made by the National Curriculum Working Party for Mathematics (DES and WO, 1988). This is inevitable; the argument here is not that this should not happen, but that we should be aware of the effects of such recontextualizations, particularly when we are considering the strategies adopted when attempting to effect change in the practices of schooling.

Two possible reorientations might be suggested on the basis of the above. These are closely related. The first is the abandonment of the notion of 'translation', in the sense of the translation of statements into practice. The close interrelationship of both knowledge and practice with context makes this so problematic as to be limited in its usefulness. Additional support for this assertion is provided by the limited success that has been experienced in the area of primary mathematics in closing the gap between rhetoric and practice, as illustrated above. Rather than the production of statements about ideal practices to be translated into the reality of classroom practice, the carry over from one field to another should perhaps be seen differently. It is obviously possible to speak about one context from within another and it is obviously possible for communications to pass from one context to another. Neither academic work nor the development of professional rhetoric nor the engagement in classroom practices are rendered futile by denial of the possibility of translation of statements generated within any one field into practices within any other. They can inform each other but, if this is to be fruitful, it should not be in terms of one dictating or prescribing the activities or practices of the other. Rather, each might provide a set of discursive resources on which to draw. The second suggested reorientation, towards a form of reflexivity, indicates how a fruitful and effective relationship might be established.

Change does take place in the teaching of mathematics in the primary school as it does in general primary practice and in the specific practices associated with other areas of the curriculum. Rather than focus on the failure of particular 'innovations' to become established at the level of the classroom, and the subsequent search for the factors that prevent this, it is being suggested that we might focus instead on what it is that provokes and sustains change in a particular context and what the specific effects of particular changes are. This reorientation points us towards forms of reflexive practice in which practitioners engage critically in examining their own practice and its effects. It is of central importance that such a process can acknowledge the specific qualities of the particular circumstances within which the teacher is working, which, of course, may include the characteristics of the teachers themselves. This might involve teachers in a form of practitioner action research (Elliott, 1991; Webb, 1989; Winter, 1989), although care must be taken not to conceive of such professional reflexion as solely enabling and monitoring the accommodation of teachers to prescriptions for change developed elsewhere. Within such work a form of dialogue needs to be set up between the various fields described above, with practitioners drawing on and engaging with theory and existing research appropriately in the critical development of their own practice, and the illumination of the practices of others in similar circumstances, as well as the possible production of more general statements to be opened to further scrutiny. This critical reflexion might involve collaboration between teachers who share particular circumstances and interests, or with others with different but related interests. Throughout this process teachers will be drawing on a wide range of resources, including the expertise of others in a variety of fields, and the theoretical and methodological resources of various intellectual traditions. This is not viewed as a comfortable process in which prejudices and viewpoints are necessarily confirmed but as a rigorous process of self-critique that constantly challenges existing assumptions, knowledge and practices, and the conditions under which these are produced. Needless to say it is not only teachers that should engage in such critical reflexion within their own field of practice: this might also be a characteristic of the work of school students (Brown and Dowling, 1989), academics (Bourdieu, 1989), other professionals working with people (Winter, 1989), and so on.

For primary mathematics teaching this turns us away from the existing position that tends to suggest that the form of action that should be taken in response to the distance between rhetoric and practice is that: (i) those who produce statements about practice should be told by practitioners to 'become realistic'; (ii) the conditions should be created so that practitioners can do the things that those who produce statements about practice tell them they should be doing. Instead we can acknowledge that as teachers we are likely to differ, for instance, in the degree of confidence we have in approaching mathematics (Buxton, 1981), not merely as an explanation of our inadequacies in the light of a set of ideal practices, but as a starting point for the development of an appropriate approach to mathematics. Other factors that shape existing practice might be viewed similarly. This has the effect of enabling teachers, in full recognition of the multitude of existing pressures and contingencies, to identify suitable points of development and change. Current initiatives designed to aid the implementation of the National Curriculum, such as the DES-designated 20-day mathematics courses, which are built around the assumption that the level of a teacher's mathematical knowledge is a key factor in the quality of primary mathematics teaching, act in direct opposition to this. This approach would also enable us to acknowledge that the practice of the primary teacher is shaped not only in relation to the general 'ideology' of primary education (Alexander, 1984) but is also cross-cut by the various 'subject cultures' of the constituent parts of the curriculum, of which mathematics is only but one.

Summary and conclusion

The authors of the papers in this book have all set out to give a considered opinion on various aspects of the National Curriculum. Within this brief I have chosen to produce neither a critique of nor a eulogy on the mathematics component of the National Curriculum. I have, rather, attempted to address some of the peculiarities of mathematics as a core subject within the primary school curriculum. The specific position of mathematics is the product of a number of factors, from its status in contemporary western culture to the particularities of the 'culture' of mathematics education. That the content of the Statutory Orders bears such close similarity to previous content guidelines and that these were produced relatively early in the process of ascribing subject-specific content to the National Curriculum also places mathematics in a distinctive position. The particular focus of this paper has been on the relationship between 'what is said' about 'good practice' in primary mathematics teaching and 'what is done'. This has served as a basis for questioning the value of a continual restatement of particular desired practices. This obviously raises further questions regarding the National Curriculum, its implementation and its relationship to existing practice.

The situation detailed above can be summarized in this way: a vast number of statements are made about what primary school teachers should do to be effective teachers of mathematics. They are made by a variety of different types of people; HMI, LEA advisers, researchers, teacher trainers, class-teachers and so on. These statements are a part of a universe of statements which constitutes what I have called the rhetoric of mathematics education, a collection of 'what is said about the teaching and learning of mathematics' by those involved, in a variety of ways, in the business of teaching mathematics. Amongst this universe of statements it is possible to discern some degree of professional consensus and unity which is manifest around the notion of 'good practice'. The circulation of images of 'good practice' takes place in a variety of ways; through various Government, local authority and professional association reports and other writing, journals and magazines, books for teachers, initial and in-service training courses, informal meetings and so on. Obviously statements about the teaching and learning of mathematics are made by people outside what we might call the 'mathematics education community'. The traces of a forcing together of particular perspectives from inside and outside this notional community can be seen in the National Curriculum Statutory Orders for mathematics. Whatever the origins of the Statutory Orders they are now established as an important element in talk and discussion about mathematics education. Resolving the content, structure and orientation of the Statutory Orders with current notions of 'good practice' is obviously of central importance in the implementation of the National Curriculum. The non-statutory guidance can be seen as an attempt to do this. 'Good practice' in the teaching of primary mathematics appears not to be widely established, however. The characteristics of 'good practice' thus act as an ideal against which the actual practices are judged and provide the dimensions along which teachers' actions are made sense of. It is also necessarily assumed that this ideal is attainable in a variety of different contexts. On the basis of these observations a radical departure from the predominant view of change in the practices of teaching mathematics is proposed. The rejection of the view that ideal practices can be non-problematically translated into actual, widespread, classroom practices, and the development of a form of reflexive practice are presented as fruitful directions to take if forms of mathematics teaching are to be developed that are appropriate to prevailing conditions and teachers who are responding to wider changes. Greater attempts are being made to support teachers in developing such reflexive approaches, such as accredited induction programmes and INSET in which 'professional writing' and small-scale practitioner research are encouraged. This contrasts with forms of INSET that attempt to disseminate particular forms of sanctioned 'good practice' which leave teachers with the problem of having to find ways of implementing this or risk not being seen as good practitioners.

The above might be seen as constituting a critique of the very notion of a National Curriculum. If it were solely this, the argument would be futile. The National Curriculum and its associated assessment procedures are with us now, albeit in ever changing form, and as such form an important part of the context within which we all work. As has been argued elsewhere (Brown, 1990) the National Curriculum will enter the domain of actual practices as yet another, albeit powerful, contingency. Thus it becomes not simply a matter of translating the contents and surrounding ephemera of the National Curriculum into particular practices, but rather the introduction of another set of pressures that lie alongside and interact with those that already act on the teacher. In this particular paper it is hoped that a case has been made for treating with caution statements like 'good practice in the teaching of primary mathematics can continue in the era of the National Curriculum'

References

Alexander, R. (1984) *Primary Teaching*. London: Holt, Rinehart and Winston.

Atkinson, P. (1985) *Language, Structure and Reproduction: An Introduction to the Sociology of Basil Bernstein*. London: Methuen.

Bernstein, B. (1990) *The Structuring of Pedagogic Discourse: Class, Codes and Control*. (Vol. 4) London: Routledge.

Bourdieu, P. (1989) *In Other Words: Essays Towards a Reflexive Sociology*. Oxford: Polity.

Brown, A.J. and Dowling, P.C. (1989) *Towards a Critical Alternative to Internationalism and Monoculturalism in Mathematics Education*. London: Centre for Multicultural Education, Institute of Education, University of London.

Brown, A.J. (in press) 'Participation, Dialogue and the Reproduction of Social Inequalities.' In: Merttens, R. and Vass, J. *Ruling the Margins: Issues in Parental Participation*. Lewes: Falmer Press.

Brown, A.J. (1990) 'From notional to national curriculum: the search for a mechanism.' In: Dowling, P.C. and Noss, R. (eds) *Mathematics Versus the National Curriculum*. Lewes: Falmer Press.

Brown, A.J. (1985) 'Primary school variation in an urban education authority: a study and discussion', unpublished MSc thesis, Polytechnic of the South Bank, London.

Brown, M. (1989) 'Make the best of it'. *Times Educational Supplement*. (29th April)

Buxton, L. (1981) *Do You Panic about Maths?* London: Heinemann.

Central Advisory Council for Education (England) (1967) *Children and their Primary Schools*. London: HMSO.

Cockcroft, et al (1982) *Mathematics Counts*. London: HMSO.

DES/HMI (1989) *The Teaching and Learning of Mathematics*. (Aspects of Primary Education Series) London: HMSO.

DES and WO (1988) *Mathematics for Ages 5 to 16: Proposals of the Secretary of State for Education and Science and the Secretary of State for Wales*. London: HMSO.

Desforges, C. and Cockburn, A. (1987) *Understanding the Mathematics Teacher: A Study of Practice in First Schools*. Lewes: Falmer Press.

Dowling, P. C. and Noss, R. (eds) (1990) *Mathematics Versus the National Curriculum*. Lewes: Falmer Press.

Dowling, P.C. (1990) 'Some notes towards a theoretical model for reproduction, action and critique'. In: Noss, R. et al (eds) *Political Dimensions of Mathematics Education: Action and Critique*. (Proceedings of the First International Conference.) Department of Mathematics, Statistics and Computing, Institute of Education, University of London.

Elliott, J. (1991) *Action Research for Educational Change*. Milton Keynes: Open University Press.

Hughes, M. (1986) *Children and Number: Difficulties in Learning Mathematics*. Oxford: Blackwell.

Küchemann, D. (1990) 'Ratio in the National Curriculum'. In: Dowling, P.C. and Noss, R. (eds) *Mathematics Versus the National Curriculum*. Lewes: Falmer Press.

Noss, R. (1990) 'A case of divide and rule?' In: Dowling, P.C. and Noss, R. (eds) *Mathematics Versus the National Curriculum*. Lewes: Falmer Press.

Noss, R., Goldstein, H. and Hoyles, C. (1989) 'Graded Assessment and Learning Hierarchies in Mathematics.' *British Education Research Journal*, Vol 15, 2, pp 109–20.

O'Reilly, D. (1990) 'Hierarchies in Mathematics: A Critique of the CSMS Study.' In: Dowling, P.C. and Noss, R. (eds) *Mathematics Versus the National Curriculum*. Lewes: Falmer Press.

Preston, M. (1987) *Mathematics in Primary Education*. Lewes: Falmer Press.

Simon, B. (1981) 'The primary school revolution: myth or reality?'. In: Simon, B. and Willcocks, J. (eds) *Research and Practice in the Primary Classroom*. London: Routledge and Kegan Paul.

Stow, M. (1988) *Mathematics Coordination: A Study of Practice in Primary and Middle Schools*. Windsor: NFER-Nelson.

Walkerdine, V. (1984) 'Developmental psychology and the child-centred peda-
    gogy: the insertion of Piaget into early education.' In: Henriques, et al *Chang-
    ing the Subject*. London: Methuen.
Walkerdine, V. (1988) *The Mastery of Reason*. London: Routledge.
Webb, R. (1989) *Practitioner Research in the Primary School*. Lewes: Falmer
    Press.
Winter, R. (1989) *Learning from Experience: Principles and Practice in Action-
    Research*. Lewes: Falmer Press.

Chapter Three
Science: Changing Directions

Jane Savage

The introduction of science as a core subject in the National Curriculum has had a great impact on the primary school and those working within it. However, it is important to examine recent developments in science teaching within the context of what science work was already being achieved in the primary school. Research was beginning to affect primary science practice and the growing body of knowledge about the subject at primary level. Researchers are continuing to develop a deeper understanding of children's progress in science thinking and how to help identify effective ways of organizing and structuring this learning. In this way we may be able to combine the strengths of the National Curriculum for science with previous and developing good practice and minimize the weaknesses existing currently both in practice and policy.

Developments before the National Curriculum
Many primary teachers lack confidence in their own ability to teach science. This is despite much work aimed at giving primary teachers confidence to provide starting points for work in the classroom and at developing structured scientific activities which build on children's initial ideas to extend scientific knowledge and understanding (ILEA, 1988; ASE, 1989, 1990). Some forms of this support are still limited. For example, there may be only one advisory primary teacher with responsibility for science in a particular LEA and books aimed at supporting teachers of infants are generally few in number and of poor quality. In addition, until recently science was not adequately studied as part of many initial primary teacher training courses. The evidence which began to be documented by HMI and the DES (DES, 1983, 1985) seemed to suggest that until the late 1980s, while there was exemplary science work going on in some primary schools, it tended to be patchy, isolated and heavily weighted towards the biological sciences; nature study, for example.

Many primary teachers have understandable reasons for not feeling confident in teaching science. In particular they may not have enjoyed their own science education while it lasted. The complex reasons for this lack of confidence are well documented (Harding, 1983) and we must ensure that these patterns, particularly as they affect girls and women, are not allowed to continue. The subject seems unfamiliar in places, appears to require a specialist knowledge and, as an essentially practical subject, has many demands associated with resourcing, organizing and managing activities in a busy primary classroom. It has not previously been well established as a traditional element of the primary curriculum and some primary teachers have therefore been able to avoid the subject and issues associated with it. Additionally it must be recognized that science is a complex subject to teach in that it consists of both process and a large body of content.

On top of all these inherent difficulties, science was also the first subject of the National Curriculum to be introduced into primary schools, so additional problems arose which were associated with becoming familiar with the structure, content and intentions of the National Curriculum as a whole, and the science document in particular. The work of Wragg et al (1989) confirms that the majority of primary teachers still lack confidence in their ability to teach science. This is a clear indication that considerable support for the generalist primary teacher is still required and that we must continue to examine the science component of initial teacher training courses. Some of the forms support could take are examined later in this chapter.

So what is good primary science and how does the science in the National Curriculum document fit into and enhance the development of the subject? Wynne Harlen in *Developing Science in the Primary Classroom* (1989) points out that one of the key elements is:

...children finding out about something through their own actions and making some sense of the result through their own thinking.

There also seems to be a consensus about science being both a method and a set of ideas, consisting of both process and content (Harlen, 1989; Driver et al, 1985). It is the tension between these two elements and what it is that is unique about science which has fuelled much of the debate on effective science teaching in the primary classroom and has had such a profound impact on the National Curriculum. Another aspect which has had a significant impact on the work which teachers plan and deliver in the primary classroom is the importance of developing a positive and enquiring attitude to science content and process, particularly when the teachers themselves lack confidence. Teachers have also been concerned about how to deliver a curriculum which is driven by the perceptions of individual children when they have to work with classes of 30 children or more. Answers to these fundamental questions continue to prove elusive although techniques such as concept mapping may provide a starting point both in finding out about initial thoughts and planning, and assessing structured, sequenced schemes of work effectively and efficiently (Novak and Gowin, 1984).

Before the introduction of the National Curriculum, the emphasis on process within science teaching was subject to fluctuation. Scientific processes, such as raising questions, investigating, making hypotheses, experimenting, predicting, interpreting, communicating and observing, were the main focus for INSET and other in-service initiatives. There was much work done on developing these process skills in a cross-curricular context. Harlen and Jelly (1989) define them further:

> Process skills are mental and physical skills used in 'processing' information about objects, events and materials that children encounter; unless these skills develop from immature 'everyday' forms to more mature and scientific forms then children are unlikely to develop scientific concepts with understanding.

However work was, and often still is, neither structured nor planned to provide children with opportunities to develop these process skills progressively. It is not uncommon to discover reception class children and 11-year-olds operating at the same level and within the same framework of teacher expectations as part of, for example, a close observation activity. This lack of progression and continuity of work in science was all too prevalent in primary schools before the introduction of the National Curriculum for science.

There has been a growing awareness and understanding of how children's scientific thinking and learning should be developed and planned. Work by Ros Driver et al (1985), the primary SPACE (Science Processes and Concept Evaluation) project based at the University of Liverpool and King's College London and the STAR project based at the Schools of Education in Liverpool and Leicester (Galton and Harlen, 1985), has led to a growing awareness of the importance of finding out what children's scientific ideas are, with the intention that the teacher can first give these ideas status and then move the child's scientific thinking on, using these initial ideas as a starting point. Unless children's initial thoughts are recognized and taken account of in the planning process so that they can be investigated, tested and carefully considered, there is a danger that there will be a mismatch between ideas and planned work and that children will not be stimulated, challenged and encouraged to become increasingly sophisticated and accurate in their scientific thinking. The key points of this constructivist view of science are that:

(1) What is already in the learner's mind matters. We need to understand why children are thinking in certain ways as well as what they are thinking in order to plan appropriate activities and experiences.

(2) Since individuals construct their own meanings of scientific concepts, we must ensure that children are given the opportunities to be actively involved in their own learning.

(3) The construction of meaning is a continuous and active process. Practical work and the opportunity to discuss and share ideas should be part of science work for children of all ages.

(4) Learning may involve conceptual change. Some topics may have to be revisited and extended through a variety of contexts and levels of complexity before conceptual change is established.

(5) The construction of meaning does not always lead to a change in belief.

(6) Learners have the final responsibility for their learning. In order for teachers to have an accurate picture of the learning of individuals, the individuals themselves should be involved in decisions influencing the planning, delivery and assessment process.

(7) Some constructed meanings are shared (CLIS, Scott, 1987). Once information on these shared meanings has been gathered it provides a useful framework to ensure that planned activities are both appropriate and manageable.

(8) Independent thought and action should be encouraged within a relevant framework provided by the teacher and the curriculum materials used.

The STAR project work already mentioned extends this constructivist model of science to include strategies for developing assessment within the classroom.

The dilemma for teachers whose confidence, knowledge and understanding in science is low is to be able to direct children's learning down relevant and appropriate routes; the National Curriculum Programmes of Study can only provide the bare bones of a framework from which to work. More detailed guidance on specific activities, procedures to elucidate what the children already know, organization and resourcing, etc are needed to support the teacher. When suggestions for activities are presented to the children as set tasks by teachers who do not understand the basic concepts behind them, both teacher and child can be led down less profitable, less appropriate or incorrect routes for investigation. This problem is compounded when some Statements of Attainment and Programmes of Study are phrased in ways which make their interpretation problematic.

Scientific attitudes are another important component of science in the primary school. These include: curiosity, respect for evidence, critical reflection, flexibility, sensitivity to living things and the environment, a willingness to take part in collaborative study and independence of thought. Together these scientific attitudes and the previously mentioned process skills form the basis for much good, open-ended, investigative, practical, primary work. But what is it that is unique to science? Scientific processes seem to embody many principles of a child-centred active learning pedagogy. The context in which these process skills are used and the nature of the content involved is critical and this is where past practice has often been weak, giving rise to shortcomings in teaching. Content was not sufficiently examined so that progression within a wide range of scientific areas was not clearly defined or achieved. This was exacerbated by a lack of teacher confidence and expertise in the sciences. So although there was a growing awareness of how scientific processes and attitudes could be developed within the primary classroom, content was a different matter. Up until the present day, and despite the impact of the National Curriculum, the science content of work that is being offered in many primary schools is biased towards the biological. It is often still fragmented, and lacking in continuity and progression throughout the primary years. As usual, the lack of teacher confidence in some scientific areas, notably energy and astronomy, coupled with a lack of resources for teachers and pupils and firm whole-school initiatives in science have all contributed to this. Where 'newer' science subjects are being introduced there is a tendency for less confident teachers to implement restrictive activities, both in terms of content and practical organization, or use published materials which encourage children to replicate teacher results or to achieve 'the one right answer'. However, guidance on content had certainly been emerging before the advent of the National Curriculum and there has been a growing awareness of the importance of progression and continuity when planning both process and content areas for study. Although this guidance and support had a limited impact on primary science practice, it is worth considering in more detail as it provides us with evidence of what was and is available to primary teachers, how the subject was developing and how the content of the National Curriculum for science fits into this developing and expanding content pattern. The arguments for and against a common content for science are well debated by Harlen (1983).

The widely known *Nuffield Junior Science Project* (1967) and the *Science 5 to 13 Project 1967–1972* were strongly based on a Piagetian model of development and contain useful strategies to help primary teachers plan interesting and relevant science activities. Although many primary schools in this country have some or all of these latter publications they have still had only a limited effect on practice and it is frequently said that they are not accessible to the non-specialist.

In 1978, the HMI's Primary Survey found that few schools had 'effective programmes for the teaching of science' and, in their review of items occurring in primary classrooms, science did not score. HMI also established in the same report that in 1978 only 17 per cent of primary schools had science post-holders. The following few years were a time of great interest in and awareness of the subject of science in the primary school. As a result, in 1983, an APU (Assessment of Performance Unit) survey reported that 90 per cent of schools stated that they included science in their curriculum and 55 per cent of schools had a science post-holder.

In 1983, DES published HMI's influential discussion paper *Science in Primary Schools*. This comprehensive document put forward four key suggestions:

(1) that content should be related to the experiences of the children;
(2) that children should understand their own physical and biological environments and understand themselves;
(3) that children should have the opportunity to progressively deepen their knowledge and understanding of scientific concepts and facts that will be useful to them as citizens;
(4) that the application of real-life problems should include technology.

There are several influential ideas here, notably the importance of science in the role it plays in our lives as adults, links between science and technology and the development of knowledge and understanding. The same document also suggested 'aspects of science that children should meet in the primary school', these being:

• the study of living things and their interaction with the environment;
• materials and their characteristics;

- energy and its interaction with materials;
- forces and their effects.

Many of the newly appointed post-holders for science were encouraged to use this document as a starting point towards the development of a whole-school science policy. This was a difficult task for many schools and science post-holders who were not always used to planning a whole-school curriculum or using the whole school year as the planning unit. The introduction of the National Curriculum has done much to reduce this fragmentation as it cannot be implemented effectively if year group teachers plan in isolation from each other. The consequential effects on planning and assessment within schools have been dramatic and beneficial.

In 1985, the DES published the booklet *Science 5 to 16: A Statement of Policy*. This document clearly stated that: 'All pupils should be properly introduced to science in the primary school.' In 1986 the Association for Science Education (ASE) launched its *Primary Science Review* and Education Support Grant (ESG). Funding provided support towards the provision of advisory primary teacher posts for science. Many of these advisory teachers had an important role to play in the spread of interest and expertise, for example, the former ILEA's JISTT (Junior and Infant Science Teacher Training) project (ILEA, 1988). Strong backing for a cross-curricular approach based on individual class teachers' topic webs or flow-charts and policies produced by individual schools were firmly established as examples of good practice. In reality the relationships between planning, delivery and assessment were weak. Links were encouraged between science specialist areas and other primary curriculum subjects. This sometimes resulted in inappropriate curricular links being made and in a fragmented science content being presented to children. The importance of content was becoming more obvious although the science content of particular activities was not always clearly identified either by teachers or by published schemes of work.

Large research projects were focusing on the development of children's thinking in science and the constructivist view of the subject area, notably the CLIS (Children's Learning In Science) project (1984), the SPACE project (1991) and more recent STAR projects (Galton and Harlen, 1985). The STAR projects' work on developing strategies to help primary teachers assess process skills in science work in their classrooms is indicative of the more recent concerns that are linked to assessment and reflect the growing study and awareness of assessment as a vital part of the teaching and learning process. Teachers are still working on strategies which help to integrate assessment into their planning, teaching and record-keeping systems, and there is far greater awareness and understanding of assessment issues since the introduction of the National Curriculum and its associated assessment requirements.

INSET courses have become longer and more complex in an attempt to meet the needs and demands of primary teachers. Currently funded models are based on study units of 20 days and there is a growing move towards accredited short courses, for example, one sixth of a diploma. The content of these courses will be considered in a later part of this chapter.

Momentum, interest and status can thus be seen to have grown rapidly over the last ten years. However, in the late 1980s Tizard et al, in their study *Young Children at School in the Inner City* (1988), recorded that practical or science work was rarely observed. There was clearly room for further improvement.

The development of the National Curriculum for Science
The Draft Orders for the science component of the National Curriculum went before Parliament in December 1988. The Working Group for science was set up in July 1987, chaired by Jeff Thompson from Bath University. Primary science specialists were heartened to learn that Ros Driver from Leeds University and Wynne Harlen from Liverpool University were to be members, with Wynne Harlen chairing the primary group. As was to prove the case with many other National Curriculum Working Groups, it was disappointing that there were not more primary class teachers or advisory teachers involved, particularly those with early years experience. This would have immediately enhanced the status of the documents in the eyes of primary practitioners and might have helped to raise the standards set for early years children. This lack of adequate early years teacher representation has resulted in an unbalanced primary curriculum. Junior aged children and their teachers have a heavy content load which realistically could have been spread throughout the whole primary age range. Expectations for junior aged children who may have had very little systematic science education or who at best will have been taught by teachers who are dealing with an unfamiliar and potentially threatening curriculum are too high in some specific areas, for example, genetics and earth sciences. There seems to be a strong move towards fragmenting the science curriculum into the traditional science subjects of chemistry, biology and physics for the older primary children. Is the

intention to introduce specialist science teaching by science graduates in the junior school? If so, it is unclear where this supply of science graduates will appear from or how they will be encouraged to teach the older children or just the sciences within the primary school. Such a move would entail a fundamental re-evaluation of primary teacher roles. There is no clear and wide ranging rationale for not including some work which can be achieved in the reception class. The anomaly is that some of the best practice in primary science can be seen in nursery and reception classrooms (Hayes, 1982). Many early years practitioners are skilled at organizing practical activities for small groups and starting from the initial ideas and interests of children. These practices which are important starting points for science work have contributed to much original and challenging science work by very young children in contexts which are meaningful to them.

In 1987 there was a move to extend the remit of the science group to include the 'new' subject of technology. This clearly had its roots in the 1983 HMI discussion paper already mentioned and, perhaps, the more prosaic view that there is much common ground between science and technology. In August 1987 a Working Group was set up to study both design and technology. The technology brief was taken up by this new group and the science Working Group concentrated on science in isolation.

The interim report for science was published in November 1987 and it was apparent that an attempt had been made to include the primary-led view of process and content being equally important within the subject. To produce a report of the detail and complexity of the interim report in just three months was a considerable achievement. It is easy to lose sight of the time constraints that the Working Group had to adhere to. It is worth reflecting that anomalies may not have arisen given a lengthier timetable, and on the reasons why more time was not available or permitted. The influences of existing good practice and the guidelines of the DES's *Science 5 to 16: A Statement of Policy* (1985) were also evident. Most primary practitioners were disappointed with the amount and prescriptive nature of content in the science document. There was an understandable fear that content overload would militate against cross-curricular delivery and that it would be difficult to cover specific areas in sufficient depth. In addition, teachers would find it difficult to develop topics or themes from children's interests. The unfamiliar nature of some of the content areas has proved to be a challenge which many primary teachers, recognizing areas of weakness in their own understanding, have been anxious to rectify. The Statutory Orders were also confusing to non-science specialists. Some of the language used is far from clear which has led not surprisingly to specific Attainment Targets being interpreted in a variety of ways. While there was an opportunity for consultation, and response to this document was invited in a prescribed form, again the time available was curtailed. It was difficult for some teachers to acquire their copies of the documents speedily and when they did it took time to understand the format, structure and sometimes language of the document. Subsequent National Curriculum documents have not had to overcome these initial hurdles.

The Final Report was published in August 1988. Again the consultation period was short and those working in primary schools and most closely concerned with implementing the proposed curriculum had only two months during one of the busiest times of the year to discuss and prepare a response. The Final Report continued to put forward a constructivist view of the subject which was somewhat at odds with the large amount of prescribed content and hierarchical system of development which it also contained. It recommended that there should be four profile components:

(1) exploration and investigation;
(2) knowledge and understanding;
(3) communication; and
(4) science in action (for secondary pupils only).

There were 22 Attainment Targets. The report did make the important distinction between planning based on Programmes of Study and assessment based on Attainment Targets and their associated Levels of Attainment. All National Curriculum subject documents which have been produced so far have failed to develop adequate strategies to organize and develop continual assessment in the classroom. It is not enough simply to state that assessment has to be done and produce guidance in ever more weighty tomes after the curriculum has been planned and implementation strategies formulated. This has been a missed opportunity to support the planning, teaching and assessment of a new science curriculum and to develop closer links between these three interrelated components. This is one reason for the success of the work produced as part of the STAR project and ASE initiatives on assessment and record keeping. It will be important to build on their findings in all forms of primary science training. This is one of the needs which seems to be

regularly identified by teachers attending INSET courses. Other important recommendations that were put forward in this Final Report include:

(1) the heavy weighting of internal teacher assessment (70 per cent);
(2) that knowledge and understanding were to have a 50 per cent weight-
     ing at Key Stages 1 and 2;
(3) that processes and knowledge (or content) should continue to be taught
     in an integrated manner.

The then Secretary of State for Education, Kenneth Baker's response to
the Report contained several far-reaching criticisms which resulted most
importantly in a narrowing down of profile components and an alternative Key Stage 4 model for children specializing in other subjects, music
for example. This seems to fit uneasily with the notion of a common
curriculum for all children aged 5 to 16. The Draft Orders that went
before Parliament in December 1988 included the amendments proposed
by Mr. Baker. There were now to be two profile components, the
exploration of science and knowledge and understanding. The weighting
for the primary phase was as follows.

	Key Stage 1	Key Stage 2
Exploration of science	50%	45%
Knowledge and understanding	50%	55%

The two models for Key Stage 4 remained.

In April 1989 the DES's document *Science in the National Curriculum*
arrived in schools. The important non-statutory guidance arrived in June
1989. It would have been more helpful to have both sets of documents
arrive together as the non-statutory guidance provides important support
in implementing the National Curriculum and in many cases helps to
make sense of it by linking teaching strategies with the planning and
delivery of content. There was some confusion on an entirely practical
level that affected access into the National Curriculum document. The
appropriate Programmes of Study for Key Stages 1 and 2 which should
have been the basis for planning the 'new' science curriculum are
'concealed' on pages 63 to 70 and they are not numbered to correspond
to the relevant Attainment Targets. It was not surprising that some
primary teachers started to plan from the Statements of Attainment
themselves, something which is still continuing in some primary schools.
Teachers who realized that the document was not set out in a helpful way

have reorganized their National Curriculum folders appropriately. These errors in the organization of the document have caused unnecessary confusion.

At present there are 14 Attainment Targets in two profile components for the primary phase.

PROFILE COMPONENT 1
Exploration of science, communication and the application of knowledge and understanding.

AT 1　*Exploration of science*

PROFILE COMPONENT 2
Knowledge and understanding of science, communication and the applications and implications of science.

AT 2　*The variety of life*
AT 3　*Processes of life*
AT 4　*Genetics and evolution*
AT 5　*Human influences on the earth*
AT 6　*Types and uses of material*
AT 9　*Earth and atmosphere*
AT 10　*Forces*
AT 11　*Electricity and Magnetism*
AT 12　*The scientific aspects of information technology including microelectronics*
AT 13　*Energy*
AT 14　*Sound and music*
AT 15　*Using light and electromagnetic radiation*
AT 16　*The earth in space*
AT 7 (Making new materials), AT 8 (Explaining how materials behave) and
　　AT 17 (The nature of science) do not apply to Key Stages 1 and 2.

Apart from the feeling that there are so many separated areas of content, one of the first reactions to the content list is that there is an inherent weakness also in separating out AT 12, the scientific aspects of information technology including microelectronics. This could have been included in profile component 1 so that it could more easily be located and used in appropriate schemes of work. This would have been a more meaningful way of using information technology. Many primary teachers have actually opted for this route, thus combining previous good practice with the new National Curriculum. Specific areas such as genetics, astronomy, forces and energy cause particular problems for teachers. These tend to be areas where adults find it hard to grasp concepts or have had little personal experience or interest in the subject together with less experience of teaching in these areas. This is certainly a powerful reason to include them for study in the primary school but at a realistic level and with strong teacher support.

Apart from arguments concerned with the structure and philosophy of all the National Curriculum documents there is the debate over the appropriateness of such a hierarchical model of learning and the fragmentation of the curriculum. Primary teachers were initially concerned with attempting to decode some of the individual Statements of Attainment. Phrases such as 'know that', 'be able to use/describe' and 'understand' have been the subject of some debate. What is heartening is to see the overlap that has emerged between lists of process skills and AT 1. The ASE's document *The National Curriculum: Making it Work for the Primary School* (1989) was also a help in its attempt to identify the similarities and differences in processes involved in English, mathematics and science. The range of content that is included in ATs 2 to 16 is interesting and comprehensive and has certainly raised interest in some specific areas (eg astronomy), previously neglected in primary schools.

Teachers and advisers initially attempted to cluster the Attainment Targets so that areas could be studied in more depth, links could be developed and models for implementation could be initiated which took account of the six times half-termly model which most primary teachers use for their planning units. Many variations of clusters have been produced. One of the earliest in London, from ILEA's North London Science Centre, is reproduced overleaf. It is interesting to note how topic or theme titles have been suggested as being related and appropriate to specific clusters. The production of topic and attainment clusters such as these had an important effect on morale, as at this stage in the development of the National Curriculum teachers began to realize more clearly that the science National Curriculum could still be delivered in a cross-curricular, topic-based manner. The North London Science Centre model was certainly enthusiastically adopted and modified by many London primary schools.

The phenomenon of the science-led curriculum developed in many primary schools. The reasons behind this are easy to comprehend. Science was a subject that was already viewed with anxiety by many primary teachers who felt more should be done; it was the first subject of the National Curriculum to be developed and, to their credit, primary teachers were anxious and willing to develop their expertise in the subject.

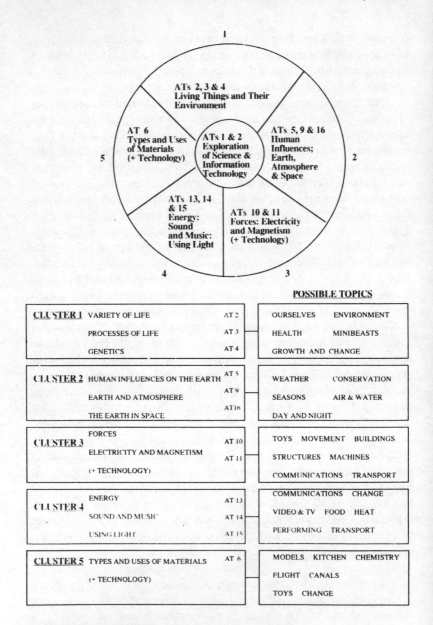

AT 1 EXPLORATION OF SCIENCE: This will be addressed at all times

AT 12 IT   THE SCIENTIFIC ASPECTS OF INFORMATION TECHNOLOGY (INCLUDING MICROELECTRONICS): This permeates all clusters. Children should be encouraged to use computers/tape recorders/turtles/videos

Science became the focus of many schools' development plans and school-based INSET and science-led topics were developed for the whole school. Many schools worked hard to integrate mathematics and English guidelines into these plans as National Curriculum reports, guidance and documents in these two subjects became available. Teachers began slowly to feel more confident in the teaching of primary science. Time and effort went into these planning exercises to considerable effect. The whole school year became the unit for planning and teachers within a school realized they had to work together to ensure continuity and progression. The opportunity for early years and junior teachers, both within individual schools and between neighbouring schools, to meet and discuss expectations, planning and acceptable standards within a structured topic has been of enormous importance in helping to improve continuity, progression and standards within and between schools as well as sharing and exchanging expertise. This valuable work has played a large part in raising standards of planning and learning in primary schools. Unfortunately the foundation subjects and particularly the humanities have suffered as a consequence of this effort. The lower status of geography and history and the nature of the National Curriculum documents have made it difficult to integrate them with science into a topic-led planning system. Although the science-led curriculum is undoubtedly a phase to be worked through, it remains to be seen whether it is possible for primary teachers to integrate all the National Curriculum subjects in any meaningful way. If it proves not to be the case this will lead to a fundamental problem. It will not be possible to hold onto an integrated cross-curricular model if the National Curriculum continues to fragment learning into separate subject compartments and integrated planning may fail. The arrangements for separate testing of the core subjects contribute further to the fragmentation of the primary curriculum.

The Non-Statutory Guidance for Science, which was published in June 1989, attempted to raise many important points which are not dealt with in the rest of the science documents. Issues such as the importance of working and planning together as a school, the role of AT 1, the importance of the Programmes of Study as a planning tool and the role of children's initial ideas in science are all included. This document has been of great use to teaching staff and has provided the basis for much staff development.

Science is now established in the primary curriculum. Concern remains with the teacher-led, closed manner in which it is being followed and with the lack of understanding in certain content areas by some teachers. Many recently published schemes continue to present stereotypical images - expect the children to follow instructions which will lead them to 'discover the one right answer' and do not encourage the children to suggest ideas or put forward testable hypotheses for themselves. The role that research into children's ideas in science can play is critical here.

Building on these recent understandings teachers have the opportunity to plan and deliver a science curriculum which builds on the children's initial ideas, developing these so that the child's scientific understanding will become more complex and incorporate the stages of development contained in the Programmes of Study as well as current scientific thinking and include opportunities to develop ideas which take account of the child's individual interests, previous experiences and upbringing. In this way we may move towards a broader and more balanced science curriculum which can incorporate positive strategies to make science even more accessible to all children and teachers, whatever their gender or background.

The future
Schools will continue to need support in planning and monitoring an agreed science curriculum. Such support takes time and resources. Some professional training days have already been devoted to this and neighbouring schools have begun to share initiatives. When Local Management of Schools (LMS) is fully introduced along with other changes in the structure and responsibilities of Local Education Authorities it is not certain how many primary advisory teachers for science will still be available, both to provide authority-wide training courses and to work with and support individual science co-ordinators and schools. The need for these specialists has never been greater. Specialist training for science co-ordinators and senior teachers to enable them to develop and lead INSET both on the science curriculum and whole school planning strategies is of great importance. LMS and the associated allocation of resources within schools also makes it crucial that money is available for resources to support teachers and the development of science within the school. Money needs to be allocated for:

(1)   Everyday classroom resources to facilitate practical work (eg a range
       of papers of different size, weight and quality, various kinds of glue,
       scissors for left- and right-handed children, plastic collecting bags,
       sticky labels, etc).

(2) Collections of interesting objects for classifying, sorting, observing and stimulating curiosity (eg seeds, fruits, springs, shells, rocks, etc).

(3) Specialist science equipment (eg thermometers, microscopes, pulleys, weighing apparatus.)

(4) Resources for keeping living plants and animals in the best possible conditions.

(5) Resources to aid communication (eg overhead projectors, tape recorders, computers with data handling and control technology software).

(6) Organizing and collating information on the school and the local environment.

(7) Organizing and collating information on the children and adults working in or associated with the school (eg parents, teachers or primary helpers with specific skills, interests or expertise).

(8) Reference books, schemes of work, activity books, cards, posters and stories for children and teachers.

Teachers seem enthusiastic and convinced of the value of science both as a mode of knowing and as a way of thinking. Demand for places on primary science INSET courses is high. Primary teachers have clearly indicated that they are willing to commit their time and energy to finding out more about how to become more effective teachers of science by enhancing their own understandings and knowledge base of the subject and by examining strategies and practice within their classrooms and schools. The range of 'twilight' courses which have been developed has increased the opportunities for professional development. Funding from LEAs, both in terms of the limited amounts that are available to support science INSET and the time consuming administration that is often associated with this funding, may affect access to these courses in the future. Whatever the length of the INSET course, there seems to be a clear pattern emerging in the support that is required. This includes:

(1) updating and extending knowledge and understanding of science content at the teachers' level;

(2) exploring the relationship between process and content (or the two profile components of the National Curriculum);

(3) exploring practical activities for use in the classroom and how to organize and resource them;

(4) exploring the links between planning, delivery and assessment;

(5) exploring and evaluating published schemes of work and other reference material and resources;

(6) sharing and reflecting on practice;

(7)   training to support science co-ordinators in initiating and supporting INSET within their own schools.

We live in a time of constant change. In May 1991 following much concern over the practical difficulties and time required in assessing the core subjects in the first run of testing, a new science document, *Science for Ages 5 to 16* (DES, 1991), was published and consultations began anew. This document attempts to 'simplify the structure so as to make assessment arrangements more manageable, not to alter the curriculum covered' (p. iii, para. 1). Five 'new' Attainment Targets are proposed:

AT1   *Scientific investigation*
AT2   *Life and living processes*
AT3   *Earth and the environment*
AT4   *Materials and their behaviour*
AT5   *Energy and its effects.*
AT1   consists of old AT1 and parts of ATs 12 and 17.
AT2   consists of old ATs 2, 3, 4 and 5.
AT3   consists of old AT9, 16 and most of 13.
AT4   consists of old ATs 6, 7 and 8.
AT5   consists of old ATs 10, 11, 14, 15 and parts of 12 and 13.

The number of Statements of Attainment has been reduced from 409 to 178. Essential strands within each New Attainment Target (NAT) have been identified.

AT 1, exploration of science, has been renamed scientific investigation, apparently because it was previously 'not well understood by parents or teachers'. I find this statement surprising given the history of science INSET and the process-led approach which has been outlined earlier in this chapter. It is unclear how these proposed changes will make it any easier for the class teacher to implement the science curriculum. It is proposed that NAT 1 will be weighted at 50 per cent both for Key Stages 1 and 2. If these proposals are accepted they are designed to come into force on 1 August 1992 (except for Y6 and Y11 children for whom it will be 1 August 1993). The mathematics National Curriculum is being similarly remodelled. It is unfortunate that during this restructuring of the National Curriculum the opportunity has not been taken to adjust levels of achievement for reception class, infant and junior aged children. Standards in certain areas, notably chemistry, are still unrealistically high and specialized. Information technology does now appear as part of NAT 1 although there is still a lack of guidance and support for teachers to enable them to implement IT effectively. It is not known what the final version of the National Curriculum will look like although substantial changes are rumoured. The present climate has renewed uncertainty for teachers and history seems to be repeating itself. An opportunity to re-evaluate the nature of the science curriculum appears to have been missed.

Teachers feel that they need more training, resources and time to integrate previous good practice and explore the potential of the National Curriculum in a way that will work for them. Much has been achieved already, some of it to the detriment of other subject areas. If our aim is to produce a balanced primary curriculum, fundamental reviews have to take place and, at present, schools and teachers do not feel they have the power to ensure that this can be achieved.

References

Alexander, R. J. (1984) *Primary Teaching*. Cassell Education.

APU (Assessment of Performance Unit) (1983) *Science at Age 11*. DES.

ASE (Association for Science Education) (1990) *Opening doors for science: Some aspects of environmental education and science in the National Curriculum for 5 to 16*. ASE and the Nature Conservancy Council.

ASE. *Primary Science Review*. Published 5 times a year: ASE, College Lane, Hatfield, Herts. AL10 9AA.

ASE (1989) *The National Curriculum - Making it Work for the Primary School*. ASE.

CLIS (Children's Learning in Science Project) (1987), Scott, P. et al, *A constructivist view of learning and teaching in science*. University of Leeds.

CLIS (1987), Needham, R. and Hill, P., *Teaching strategies for developing understanding in science*. University of Leeds.

DES (1978) *Primary Education in England: A Survey by HM Inspectors of Schools*. HMSO.

DES (1983) *Science in Primary Schools*. DES.

DES (1985) *Science 5 - 16 : A Statement of Policy*. HMSO.

DES (1989) *Science in the National Curriculum*. HMSO.

DES (1991) *History in the National Curriculum*. HMSO.

DES (1991) *Geography in the National Curriculum*. HMSO.

DES (1991) *Science for Ages 5 to 16*. HMSO.

Driver, R. et al (1985) *Children's Ideas in Science*. Milton Keynes: Open University Press.

Galton, M. and Harlen, W. (eds) (1985) *STAR project: Observing Activities, Practical Tasks, Written Tasks*. Paul Chapman Publishing Ltd.

Harding, J. (1983) *Switched Off: The Science Education of Girls*. Schools Council/Longmans.

Harlen, W. (1983) 'Does Content Matter in Primary Science?' In: Richards, S.C. and Holford, D. (eds) *The Teaching of Primary Science: Policy and Practice.* The Falmer Press.

Harlen, W. (1985) *Teaching and Learning Primary Science.* Paul Chapman Publishing Ltd.

Harlen, W. and Jelly, S. (1989) *Developing Science in the Primary Classroom.* Oliver and Boyd.

Hayes, M. (1982) *Starting Primary Science.* Edward Arnold.

ILEA (1988) *Helping Children to Become Scientific.* ILEA Publications.

Novak, J.D. and Gowin, D.B. (1984) *Learning How To Learn.* Cambridge: Cambridge University Press.

Nuffield Junior Science Project. (1967) Collins.

Richards, C. and Holford, D. (eds) (1983) *The Teaching of Primary Science: Policy and Practice.* The Falmer Press.

Science 5 - 13 Project 1967-1972. (1972) The Schools Council/Macdonald.

SPACE (Science Processes and Concept Exploration) Project Research Reports. (1991) Liverpool University Press.

Tizard, B. et al (1988) *Young Children at School in the Inner City.* Lawrence Erlbaum Associates Ltd.

Wragg, E. et al (1989) 'Teachers' worries over National Curriculum.' *Junior Education* 13 (6).

Chapter Four
Design and Technology

Marilyn Metz

The original terms of reference for the National Curriculum Design and Technology Working Group expressed the Government's wish that clear objectives be set for the knowledge, skills and understanding that pupils should be expected to have acquired in technology. Originally, primary technology had been part of the brief of the Science Working Group, and the Design and Technology group was asked to build upon the work of the Science group but was also required, in its final report, to submit recommendations for Attainment Targets and Programmes of Study in design and in information technology for primary age pupils, which were to supplement the recommendations of the science group.

The final Orders (interestingly entitled *Technology in the National Curriculum* (DES/WO, 1990) and yet referring to Attainment Targets and Statements of Attainment for both design and technology capability) represent a somewhat different document from that which might have been envisaged from the original brief. This document establishes Attainment Targets and Programmes of Study relating to all four Key Stages in what is identified, albeit unclearly, as the curriculum area of design and technology. In one respect, the way in which primary design and technology appears to have just evolved, as opposed to having been identified as existing (in whatever form) at the outset, reflects the difficulty of identifying it as a distinct curriculum area within primary education. In another, the fact that it is extraordinarily difficult to establish the existence of design and technology as a 'subject', coupled with the fact that it is now a legal requirement that it be taught, may well contribute to some interesting and productive ways in which a subject-based National Curriculum might be interpreted in the primary sector.

The nature of design and technology
Before examining this potential it is important that the special nature of design and technology be examined in some detail. The non-statutory

guidance accompanying the Orders speaks of design and technology being 'an activity which spans the curriculum' (DES/WO, 1990). It also refers to design and technology as 'a way of working'. These statements would appear to support a view of design and technology as being primarily concerned with process, and the applications of that process across the spectrum of the curriculum. The same guidance, however, highlights what could be considered a fundamental problem in that design and technology is also specifically referred to as a new subject. Indeed, by publishing the Statutory Orders for Technology before all other foundation subjects, the Government has prioritized its values clearly, a process which has been developing in education generally over a period of more than ten years (Lawton, 1988).

Not only is there a potential tension between design and technology as 'process' and as 'subject', it is also important to be aware of the fact that the relationship between design and technology is in itself not a simple one. The Working Group's Interim Report stated that elements of design and aspects of technology overlap, and that many of the former activities will include the latter, and vice versa. The Statutory Orders make no mention of the relationship between design and technology, and there is very little discussion in the non-statutory guidance apart from a brief commentary on Attainment Target 2 (Generating a Design). This Attainment Target focuses on developing a design proposal, but also includes aspects of modelling which imply the utilization of technology.

Harrison et al (1989), quoted in McCormick (1990), argue that elements of design and aspects of technology do not necessarily overlap. Their contention is that the relationship between design and technology will differ, depending on what kind of project is actually being attempted. In some situations, particularly that of constructing a prototype, it is possible that technology will become part of the design process and be seen as separate from the creation of a product. This can be illustrated by considering the construction of a building or a bridge, when model-making, involving technology, will be a part of designing. In other situations, prototypes can be seen also as products; for instance, making a toy. In this case, design can be seen to overlap with technology, whereas in the former situation design may be identified as distinct from technology, but including elements of it.

A closer inspection of the Attainment Targets detailed in the Orders shows that process, and process skills, are fundamentally important elements in the model of design and technology that the orders support. Attainment Target 1 is concerned with pupils' ability to identify and articulate the needs and opportunities for design and technology-oriented activities within varying contexts; Attainment Target 2 addresses the design process; Attainment Target 3 centres on planning and making, while Attainment Target 4 highlights the process of evaluation. These four targets are linked to form Profile Component 1. Attainment Target 5 relates to information technology and itself is the sole component of Profile Component 2. Indeed, the Statutory Orders also separate the Programmes of Study for Attainment Targets 1 to 4, and that for information technology, as well as there being separate non-statutory guidance. A discussion of the special nature of information technology within the National Curriculum is undertaken later in this chapter.

Looking at Attainment Targets 1 to 4, there are clear links in this structure with established targets in science (AT 1) and mathematics (ATs 1 and 9), and there are also important connections with literature that has examined the nature of the problem-solving process in varying curricular contexts (Polya, 1957; Mason, 1982; Harlen, 1985). Now this identification of design and technology process with problem-solving in a scientific or mathematical context has been legitimately described as 'facile' by the National Curriculum Art Working Group in its Interim Report (DES, 1991). Although it may justifiably be claimed that equating the processes involved in design and technology activities with those inherent in scientific and mathematical problem-solving will dilute meaning, it is, however, important that the parallels and connections be investigated further, and not summarily dismissed. The following paragraph attempts a tentative and somewhat simplistic analysis.

Despite the important differences between process-centred approaches to differing curriculum areas, there are important common features which may be seen as strands running parallel to each other in each of the separate Statutory Orders. These strands can also be seen as being potentially interwoven, and this view may well be a more productive one when attempting to develop an integrated approach to the delivery of the National Curriculum in the primary school. Identifying these common features may well mean that it is possible to see the content of the Technology Orders as a framework that would make some cohesive sense of apparently varying National Curriculum demands. Looking at the first four Technology Attainment Targets as a unit, we can identify a process which involves establishing the existence of needs, designing, planning and creating so that these needs can be satisfied, together with the essential element of evaluation. Within the design and technology domain, engaging in this process must take account of the need to reconcile many different factors, each of which needs to be considered not only in isolation, but in relation to each other. It is also important that the design itself needs to be an integrated whole (Design Council, 1987). Successful management of all of the constraints is therefore an essential part of the design process within a technology context. A further important feature of design within a technology context is that it does not provide us with the only answer, but one alternative amongst many. This alternative may have reconciled the various constraints in a way that will not be imitated by other solutions, which in themselves may also be acceptable solutions as well as containing some form of compromise in satisfying potentially contradictory constraints. Acceptance of a solution will not only depend upon the degree to which it satisfies the original criteria, but will also be closely connected with the values inherent in the brief. Within a mathematical context, however, it could be argued that the problem-solving process takes a slightly different form. Here the cycle consists of identifying a problem, devising strategies that will be effective in finding a solution, implementing these strategies and checking whether a solution has been found to the original problem; a similar pattern to that described above for design and technology. The identification of the problem and the development of strategies to solve it may, however, involve simplification of the problem, so that, for instance, a solution for a special case is sought at first, and only when that has been successfully achieved is the original problem approached. Indeed, this is often the course prescribed (Polya, 1957). It may well be that such simplification also takes place within the early stages of the designing and making process. What distinguishes mathematical problem-solving, however, is that after simplifying and then generalizing, successful solutions to a problem will reach the same end, but possibly by different routes. Scientific investigation can be seen as somewhat different again. The pattern of identifying the problem, developing and implementing a strategy, followed by evaluating, can be seen as similar to the cycle within both mathematics and design and technology. Unlike the technology-oriented process, however, finding a solution often involves not only identifying variables, but also controlling their effects. Scientific problem-solving can be seen as a possible part of the designing and making sequence, taking place in the early stages of development of an idea, perhaps when models and/or prototypes are constructed in order to investigate the effects of a specific variable. Ultimately, however, the compromise needed in order to achieve a satisfactory design/technology solution will mean that all variables need to be taken into account rather than controlled.

Implications for primary school practice

The common threads which can be seen might be identified tentatively as being related to exploration, discovery and creation and the need to communicate with other people about each of these. Donaldson (1978) paints a picture of good primary education with these three features at its centre. Many other writers have addressed the problem of identifying the essential elements of good primary practice; this is not the place for a detailed examination of these debates. It has, however, been argued by many that active exploration, coupled with involvement in what is relevant to the learner, is central to the existence of good practice. Behind this emphasis lies the assumption that the child is the central consideration; indeed, since Plowden in 1967, the essence of good primary practice has been that it is child-centred. If the child is to remain at the centre, then certain features of the education process become important. Blyth (1988) argues that the central element is that of informality which is in itself a complex concept, involving pedagogy, curriculum, organization, evaluation and personal style.

National Curriculum demands have had a major effect on informality of curriculum and of evaluation. Curriculum content is now legally prescribed in all core and most foundation subjects and, although themes and topics are still most often the vehicles for curriculum content in primary schools, far more consideration of content is now essential. It is necessary to identify not only how children will be learning, but what they will be expected to know and understand. It could therefore be argued that the National Curriculum has made informality of curriculum more difficult to achieve than in pre-1988 days. In a similar way, informality of evaluation has been considerably restricted, through the introduction of standardized approaches to assessment. Bernstein (1975) would perhaps argue that these restrictions upon informality of curriculum and evaluation are not necessarily to be mourned. Establishing explicit content for curriculum and criteria for evaluation have arguably made primary school practice more accessible; indeed, this is one of the fundamental tenets underlying the educational reform that has taken place in the last few years.

Informality of personal style is perhaps one aspect of primary school practice least affected by recent legislative changes, although teachers have commented unfavourably on the effects that National Curriculum demands have had upon the ways in which they interact with the children in their care, particularly with regard to the maintenance of productive relationships with children during periods of formal assessment. Personal style however, is perhaps a less relevant consideration in this present context.

The most interesting aspects of Blyth's analysis of present primary practice are those of the informalities of pedagogy and of organization, and it is these that bear more consideration in the light of the Technology Orders. Within the primary classroom, the informalities of pedagogy and organization are represented by features such as opportunities for structured play, active involvement with materials and ideas, and flexibility in the arrangement of the physical, social and temporal structures. Children are able to engage with activities, if necessary over an extended period of time and in small groups. They will have independent access to tools and materials, be they paper and pencil, construction materials or computers. This child-oriented environment is created so that access to learning and opportunities for effective teaching are maximized. One of the major aims is that learning be contextualized through first-hand experiences.

It is not possible here to examine every aspect of good primary practice within the framework of design and technology, but by looking at the Technology Orders for Key Stages 1 and 2 within the context of two familiar kinds of classroom activity, an attempt will be made to illuminate connections between the content of the document and some aspects of good practice which will support National Curriculum demands rather than be undermined by them.

One of the fundamental features of the early school years is its emphasis on the role of play in a child's development. The presence of play activities, usually structured in some way by the teacher, is commonplace in nursery and infant classes, although it is less often encountered in the junior school. Play is a complex concept and defies straightforward definition. No attempt to define it will be made here; readers are referred to the extensive literature on the subject, competently detailed in such books as Moyles' (1989) *Just Playing?*. Some of the important features of play include the fact that it is a necessary part of satisfactory human existence, that it cannot be clearly distinguished from work, and that it is most productively viewed as a process. Moyles (1989) emphasizes the importance of viewing play as a process, and supports Bruner's contention that play is 'an approach to action, not a form of activity' (Bruner, (1977), quoted in Moyles, (1989)). It is here, taking the view that play is an approach to action, that it is possible to see links between play and designing and making as a way of working, and thus to make fruitful connections between play and what is detailed in the Technology Statutory Orders. In order to establish these connections, it is also important to consider what kind of play takes place.

As mentioned above, play activities are often structured by the class teacher in her/his choice of materials and environment for the children to explore. Creating a structured play situation implies that there is an alternative, namely, that of unstructured play. Moyles (1989) argues that this distinction is not a particularly fruitful one to make. Play is always structured by the environment in which it takes place and the materials that are available to use, whether a teacher has made active decisions or not. The kind of building attempted with bricks will depend on factors that include how many bricks are available, what sort of surface is available to build on and how well the bricks stack on each other and on the surface. More potentially useful to teachers, and to a consideration of the role of play in fostering design- and technology-oriented thinking, is an approach to play that identifies it as either free or directed. Moyles (1989) identifies a spiral which incorporates free and directed play at different stages within the play process in the classroom, where an initial period of free play is followed by an intervention that is designed to direct the play, which in turn leads to a new and possibly different period of free play. The role of the teacher rather than any specific content is what is important here. Directed play implies intervention of some kind, but in order that the activity is still able to be seen as play, this intervention needs to enable the child to retain ownership of the play (Coghill, 1989).

One feature of many play activities is the potential for exploring the nature and properties of materials, whatever the context in which the play takes place. Using sand, modelling with clay or building with wooden bricks all open up the possibility of discovering what can and cannot be achieved with these materials. 'Working with materials' is specified within the Programmes of Study for all four Key Stages of technology, and a familiarity with the nature and properties of many different kinds of materials is an essential prerequisite to successful designing and making. This familiarity may be developed best through using the materials in contexts in which the child has control, and can feel safe in her/his explorations (Coghill, 1989). It is here that familiarity with the Programmes of Study for Key Stages 1 and 2 will help teachers to focus on and exploit the design and technology potential of play situations, together with the need to provide a real quality of independence and choice for the child, as opposed to an apparent one.

Coghill (1989) defines design as having to do with 'taking action and with imagining and considering what actions could or might be taken. ...the intention is to re-order, change or alter spatial or physical reality for a specific purpose or idea.' Baynes (1989), in his definition of design, emphasizes this element of imagination. Without the ability to imagine changes, the potential for design does not exist. Being able to imagine is also an integral part of all kinds of play. Without opportunities to develop imagination, an individual's ability to design may well be sorely restricted.

The second kind of activity commonly encountered as part of good primary practice is the provision of varied opportunities for children to make models. Many different model-making materials are standard provisions in classrooms, and each has its own potential as well as limitations. Junk modelling, sometimes referred to as model-making with 'found' materials, is something that takes place throughout the primary age-range. Most children will have created something in this way before they leave the primary sector; it may have been a wheeled vehicle from soft drink cans and boxes, or a puppet from a paper bag. They will have been actively involved in making something that they have chosen to create. Indeed, this emphasis on making is a significant feature of present primary practice. It is, however, not only the making but also the context in which the making occurs that is important, together with the child's developing ability to reflect upon the processes involved in creating. The actual making of a model could perhaps be seen as a less important part of the process, the emphasis needing to be on other aspects of the cycle in order that design- and technology-oriented development may best take place.

Various writers have attempted to establish what elements are important in the designing and making cycle. Dunn and Larson (1990) speak of investigation, invention, implementation and evaluation, and see these four aspects as integrally related. Within each stage the whole cycle is repeated, so that the model becomes a complex one. The Williams and Jinks (1985) model, the 'Design Line', starts with a problem or need, and continues through early ideas and research and development. This, in turn, leads to selecting a potential solution, making, evaluating and finally accepting, altering or rejecting this solution. There are obvious parallels between these two descriptions of designing and making. The Technology Orders reflect this approach. Attainment Target 1 is concerned with identifying needs and opportunities within various contexts: AT 2 concerns itself with design specification and development; AT 3 deals with the process of making, while AT 4 addresses issues of evaluation and communication.

The implications of this model for classroom practice are diverse, and can only be outlined here. It is obvious, however, that making must be seen as part of a potentially cyclical process, and not only as an end in itself. It is not enough to have children model-making with 'found' materials. The model-making must be embedded within a much broader framework, which encompasses planning, designing and evaluating. What model-making in itself does offer is opportunities to explore materials and their properties and to make increasingly informed decisions about the appropriateness of materials for certain purposes, and experience of handling different tools and becoming competent in their use.

The position of information technology
The special position of information technology within the Technology Orders was briefly referred to earlier in the chapter. Information technology appears as a separate Attainment Target and also as a distinct profile component and, as such, seems, from the structure of the statutory document, to have a specific but somewhat separate position under the broad umbrella of technology. The position is further complicated by the fact that aspects of information technology are included within documents relating to the core curriculum subjects as well as being addressed specifically in the technology document. Indeed, an entire Attainment Target (AT 12) in the 1989 Science Statutory Orders is devoted to the scientific aspects of information technology. References are also made in the English and the Mathematics documents to the use of information technology in various forms.

There is no definition of information technology offered within the statutory section of the Technology Orders, nor is there one within the non-statutory guidance. It is stated in the guidance that information technology is a cross-curricular skill and 'should be taught as an integral part of most foundation subjects in primary... schools' (DES/WO, 1990). The emphasis is definitely in favour of a cross-curricular approach to information technology. Although brief reference is made to micro-electronic devices in general, the overwhelming and not always implicit emphasis, both within the document and the guidance, is upon computers and their uses. Perhaps the absence of a clear definition of information technology is something to be welcomed. Technological developments seem to use a different kind of time from that in which we live; today's hypothetical possibilities rapidly become yesterday's established facts. It could be argued that by avoiding a firm definition of what information technology involves, the technology document enables future developments to be included within its framework. There is, however, a need to move towards incorporating many differing kinds of technological development within the remit of information technology. At best, information technology can be viewed as an umbrella term which covers such items as calculators, programmable toys and robots, interactive video and electronic mail. In this context, emphasis on computers and their applications would seem to be unnecessarily restricting, and, although, as mentioned above, the Statutory Orders do not provide an explicit definition of information technology, the implied emphasis on computers is perhaps a cause for some concern.

Looking at the information technology component of the Technology Orders in more detail, it is important to note that the emphasis is placed on the use of generic computer applications rather than content-specific software; databases and word-processing are both mentioned in the examples offered within the Statutory Orders, and in fact databases are the only application specifically mentioned within the text of the Orders. This emphasis on content-free applications is to be welcomed as acknowledgement of the role of computers as a tool for learning within the primary curriculum as a whole. There are, however, important implications here in relation to the practical implementation of this element of the Technology Orders. Using generic software effectively in the classroom involves a large commitment of time; coming to terms with using a word processor as a tool that facilitates the writing process does not happen overnight, neither for teacher nor child. Access is needed on a continuous basis rather than for one short period of time during a week. This highlights the problem of availability of computers in primary schools. Many schools are not able to provide one machine for each class of children, and so the computing facilities in any one school are often seen as a scarce resource. The major criterion in utilizing resources that are scarce is often considered to be that of fairness, and fairness is commonly interpreted as the need for each user to have access to equal amounts of time. On this principle, a primary school with ten classes and four computers would offer each class the use of a computer for two days a week. Good primary practice relies upon children working at their own pace, and having access to the necessary tools at the times when they need to use them. What happens on the three days when the computer is not available and children need to work on what they have already started to compose on a word-processor? In this situation, which is all too common in the primary sector, what tends to happen is that when the computer is available, it is used as an electronic typewriter to produce fair copy, and the full power of word-processing is not available to the children. A similar situation may well occur when other generic software is used. A whole-school policy on computer use which takes into account not only fairness but also effective use of equipment within the learning environment is an essential part of providing access to National Curriculum requirements. This approach must also take into account the professional development of staff. The overall financial implications are considerable, and need to be addressed urgently.

Conclusion

This chapter has attempted to examine the Technology Orders in the light of present primary classroom practice. Put simply, the message here has been that, in order to deliver the Technology National Curriculum, primary practice first needs to be viewed through 'design and technology spectacles'. In this way the design and technology process can be seen as being embedded within ordinary classroom activities. Indeed, in identifying and capitalizing upon the design and technology potential within everyday classroom activities, these very activities may themselves be enhanced as learning experiences. This is not an easy task, and requires large commitments of time from teachers, continuing in-service support, and recognition of the fact that adequate provision implies considerable financial investment. For design and technology to maintain the high profile it has been given, careful thought, followed by rapid action on these needs, is essential.

References

Baynes, K. (1989) 'The Basis of Designerly Thinking in Young Children.' In: A. Dyson (ed.) Bedford Way Papers 36: *Looking, Making and Learning: Art and Design in the Primary School*. London: Institute of Education.

Bernstein, B. (1975) *Class, Codes and Control, Vol. 3: Towards a Theory of Educational Transmissions*. London: Routledge and Kegan Paul.

Blyth, A. (1988) 'Introduction.' In: A. Blyth, (ed.) *Informal Primary Education Today: Essays and Studies*. Lewes: The Falmer Press.

Coghill, V. (1989) 'Making and Playing, the Other Basic Skills: design education for the early years.' In: A. Dyson (ed.) Bedford Way Papers 36: *Looking,*

Making and Learning: Art and Design in the Primary School. London: Institute of Education.

DES/WO (1990) *Technology in the National Curriculum.* London: HMSO.

DES/WO (1991) *National Curriculum Art Working Group Interim Report.* London: DES.

Design Council (1987) *Design and Primary Education: The Report of the Design Council's Primary Education Working Party.* London: The Design Council.

Donaldson, M. (1978) *Children's Minds.* London: Fontana Press.

Dunn, S. and Larson, R. (1990) *Design Technology: Children's Engineering.* Lewes: The Falmer Press.

Harlen, W. (1985) 'Why science? What science?' In: W. Harlen (ed.) *Primary Science... Taking the Plunge.* Oxford: Heinemann Educational.

Lawton, D. (1988) 'Ideologies of Education.' In: D. Lawton and C. Chitty (eds) Bedford Way Papers 33: *The National Curriculum.* London: Institute of Education.

Mason, J, with Burton, L. and Stacey, K. (1982) *Thinking Mathematically.* London: Addison-Wesley.

McCormick, R. (1990) 'Technology and the National Curriculum: the creation of a "subject" by committee?' *The Curriculum Journal,* Vol.1, No.1, pp. 39-51.

Moyles, J. (1989) *Just Playing?: The Role and Status of Play in Early Childhood Education.* Milton Keynes: Open University Press.

National Curriculum Council (1990) *Technology Non-Statutory Guidance - Design and Technology Capability.* York: National Curriculum Council.

National Curriculum Council (1990) *Technology Non-Statutory Guidance - Information Technology Capability.* York: National Curriculum Council.

Polya, G. (1957) *How To Solve It.* Princeton: Oxford University Press.

Williams, P. and Jinks, D. (1985) *Design and Technology 5 - 12.* Lewes: The Falmer Press.

Chapter Five
Humanities: Round the World and Through the Ages

Caroline Heal

Introduction

Shaping the beginning of what I want to say, I am aware of some inevitabilities. This National Curriculum calls for a response. So, then, the structure of our response in this book echoes in part the structure of the National Curriculum itself. As the agenda has been set progressively, subsequent discussion adopts those terms of reference and works from those assumptions. The tone may be critical, but the challenge is not fundamental. Apparently there is indeed a broad consensus. We are on our way towards a National Curriculum for statutory schooling defined in terms of the traditional subjects. Provocatively, the first phase of implementation is being accomplished in that sphere where the traditions of subject teaching have the least influence. It seems an important moment.

There has been a great deal of change in a short period of time. Yesterday's radical proposals are today's status quo. As the momentum gathers for geography and history, it may appear odd to try to treat them together in a chapter with a 'humanities' focus, but the intention is threefold. Firstly, I want to emphasize the need to approach the planning of the primary curriculum as a whole. Secondly, and more contentiously, I want to make claims for the special potential of some parts of the curriculum to 'humanize', and thirdly I want to signal the importance of the cross-curricular themes in this respect.

It is important not to be complacent about existing practices, or uncritical of current curriculum models, but it is also important to trace the paths that curriculum development has taken in the past and to recognize that constructive change, however inspired, must come about through development by teachers of their existing classroom practice.

I want to argue that this is an important opportunity for primary practitioners, howsoever involved with children in the classroom, to reclaim their professional territory and to develop a critical dialogue, both within the profession, and with the bureaucracy that organizes it, so that the National Curriculum can be properly subject to professional review and evaluation. Teachers must be the key agents in this if new practices are to be developed and morale restored.

This process has already begun, of course, but the publication of the Statutory Orders for History and for Geography (DES, 1991) remind us forcibly of the urgency. This curriculum is reaching critical mass, most particularly at Key Stage 2. At the same time, implementation is sufficiently underway for us to begin to have some experience on which to build the process of review.

The decision to describe the curriculum as subjects, and then to set up subject Working Groups, with no overarching brief to consider links with other parts of the curriculum, and setting them staggered reporting dates so that their deliberations have been received in series, has had its effect. To be sure, primary teachers have been repeatedly assured that cross-curricular ways of working need not be undermined by the structure of the National Curriculum, but discussions about how ways of working can be articulated have been forced into suspended animation by the 'serial' reporting of the subject groups. The cross-curricular themes, supposedly an insurance against the narrowing of the curriculum and the erosion of important areas of work, remain in constant danger of marginalization. The historians of the curriculum, in the future, may point to positive benefits from the way in which primary teachers have had to unravel the curriculum, and focus on its constituent parts for a period, before they can begin to find models for unifying it satisfactorily as an experience for the children. In the meantime, the experience for primary teachers has been less than comfortable. Initially, the need to accommodate the National Curriculum for science dominated planning. Now history and geography threaten to tip us into a predictable but unseemly jostle for curriculum time. In this atmosphere of crisis, drastic solutions are being proposed to 'new' problems. 'Paper and pencil' tests will simplify the administration of Standard Assessment Tasks - specialist teachers in primary schools will remedy deficiencies in expertise. Paradoxically, the pace of change both stimulates and inhibits debate. However, despite our collective astonishment at a curriculum described as subjects, dictated by a bureaucracy seemingly oblivious of much contemporary curriculum theory and practice, much interesting work has been done by the subject Working Groups.

In the case of history and geography, this work has a wider context as an episode in a complex and long-running debate about the contested territory of 'humanities' (Proctor, 1987; Blyth, 1990). The institutional site for this debate has been the curriculum of the secondary school. The development of integrated humanities courses has been variously applauded or vilified; the debates have resumed recently, focused around the fate of geography and history at Key Stages 3 and 4. However, few 'primary' voices have been heard in these debates. Neither a conception of humanities, nor of specialist subject work in history or in geography, have had a clear profile in the primary curriculum. Its recent tradition has been dominated by the preoccupation with curriculum 'integration' (Alexander, 1984). This being so, it is interesting to consider whether the best case for the place of humanities in the primary curriculum is made by arguing for the constituent disciplines, invoking their distinctiveness, or by drawing on their commonality and the links that allow them to be grouped philosophically in argument or pragmatically in the practice of curriculum. I want to take advantage of both possibilities, but also to emphasize the importance of the much wider debate about the organization of the curriculum as a whole, especially in the primary phase.

Humanities in the curriculum

The Humanities have a special and distinct importance. Language and mathematics have been given central place in the curriculum because they are powerful symbolic systems which both influence and express human experience. Science, elevated now to membership of a curriculum trinity, has built its claim in an atmosphere of moral panic about our national standing in a world where technological advance has become a measure of social well-being. It claims a special methodology for developing our understanding of the workings of the world. But language and mathematics are 'vehicle' subjects for the expression of other truths. We think of them as necessary to the development of understanding about the world, but the point of education is to seek to understand and influence the human condition. Philip Taylor writing in his preface to *Humanities in the Primary School* (Campbell and Little, 1990) states it plainly: 'It is the humanities that provide the meaningful context for much that is taught and learnt.' The humanities is that part of the curriculum which focuses on people, their thoughts, feelings, beliefs and actions, in times past, present and future, and wherever they may be. Its interest is compulsive – it is first and foremost about ourselves. (How exasperating that the ubiquitous class topic of that title should so regularly consist of cataloguing the 'senses' and compiling body measurements!)

The development of a methodology of primary science education has been accelerated with the help of substantial funding so that, over a short space of time, a new orthodoxy has been established, the hallmarks of which are the manipulation of concrete things and the observation of effects in the classroom, with an emphasis on what children can observe, speculate about, deduce and record themselves. Teachers' knowledge is to be built up, not to prepare them for an instructor's role, but so that they may be aware of whither an investigation tends, and distinguish a promising line of enquiry from a dead end (Harlen, 1985).

The 'material' for study in the humanities is of a different sort, but the methodology employed to explore it is no less rigorous. Kitson Clark (1967), writing of history, has argued that 'a reasoned hypothesis based on a careful consideration of evidence which has been tested critically and systematically might be considered to have a claim to be called *scientific*. Indeed, it seems that much historical work has a better title to that question-begging adjective than much theorising that assumes it as a matter of right.' In history, for instance, the characteristic procedures require the same precision in evaluating evidence, but the evidence is of a different kind. The evidence is of human actions in the past, and human actions are influenced by the beliefs and values of human actors as well as by aspects of physical circumstances.

From the constituencies of the humanities we can find justification for a pre-eminent place in the curriculum. A historical perspective is a necessary part of understanding any aspect of the present, and much better made explicit. 'It is for this reason that it is odd to ask what use history has, or why it should be learnt. If our knowledge of the present is never an *instantaneous* knowledge, and brings with it willy-nilly some substantive conception of the past, then to be historically ignorant is just to be ignorant' (Dickinson et al, 1984). And further, 'thinking about the past must be part of our concern for the present and future. In this way history contributes to the personal development of ourselves and our pupils, and to the general education of us all' (DES, 1985). It offers an awareness of the nature of evidence, an appreciation of change and continuity, an understanding of cause, the possibility (much misunderstood) of historical empathy, an ability to pose historical questions, and a sense of chronology and time (DES, 1985).

A concern for the future has been an explicit aspect of recent thinking in geography also, reflected in the reports of the Geography Working Group, which, with the widely welcomed emphasis on environmental geography and the strong statement of the importance of geography in multicultural education and links to education for economic awareness and for citizenship, share the growing concern that geographical education should encourage the development of personal commitment and social and moral responsibility.

An approach to the place of humanities that is based on special pleading for distinctive perspectives may appeal to 'specialist' interests and have the doubtful virtue of coincidence with the pattern of the National Curriculum. It exploits legitimate claims. However, it ignores several strands in the development of work across a range of related subject areas, including not just history and geography, but social studies and political education also, and the full range of cross-curricular themes.

Campbell (Campbell and Little, 1989) identifies three important projects as exemplars of this broader approach: the Schools Council Project, the work of Lawton et al (1971), and the work of Alan Blyth at Liverpool (1976) all developed some key social concepts that could provide an organizing framework for a curriculum for the middle years. The work attempted to maintain the distinctiveness of the disciplines within a unifying framework. The ambitious project MACOS, (Man: A Course of Study), was a significant attempt by the American psychologist Jerome Bruner (1966), to frame a curriculum based on a theory of learning. And, more recently, the Inner London Education Authority (ILEA, 1980) in its series of Curriculum Guidelines, also identified the concepts, skills and attitudes to be fostered by a 'social studies' curriculum which 'is about people and their relationships in society... it is concerned to develop children's critical awareness and understanding. It does this by using their everyday experiences of social life as a starting point, and then ... the understandings children have of their immediate world are explored and extended in wider studies.' (ILEA, 1980, quoted in Campbell and Little, 1989).

There are other identifiable traditions, too, which have made a significant contribution to the development of primary work. The 'World Studies 8-13 Project' grew out of earlier work by the World Studies Project, founded by members of an all-party Parliamentary group at Westminster (Hicks, 1990). Its emphasis on education for an awareness of global issues and the links between local, national and international dimensions of change, and its endorsement of active learning methods have been influential, especially within some LEAs.

Within this tradition, the work of the Development Education agencies, such as Oxfam, and the regional initiatives embraced by the National Association of Development Education Centres in offering

in-service work for teachers and encouraging the production of innovative teaching materials, continues to develop. Some of the best material
has been planned as a stimulus for developing critical analysis of taken-
for-granted media images of people, places and events that offer such
powerful and often unchallenged constructions of the world. This 'media
studies' approach also has its own history and theoretical base, recently
made more accessible to teachers through the publication of the BFI/DES
document, *Primary Media Education: A Curriculum Statement* (1989).

All these groups are responding to the proposals for the National
Curriculum, and showing how their work can continue and develop, not
just in relation to conceptions of history and geography teaching, but
across the whole curriculum. The key elements in all these projects are
the aim to develop children's critical awareness of the social world
around them, their ability to challenge the taken-for-granted, and the
importance and legitimacy of the child's own experience as a starting
point.

Humanities concerns itself with human beliefs and actions, and its
enterprise is to seek out the threads of explanation for human decisions
that have shaped the way the world was, is, and will be. Most importantly,
human decisions only make sense within particular perspectives of the
world, particular ideologies, which could, under other circumstances, be
different. It is this possibility of alternative outcomes that carries with it
the richest gift for the student of the humanities – the inescapable
inference that ordinary human actors participate in decision-making,
actively or passively, and at levels from the domestic, to the local,
societal to global.

This is the special potential for the contribution to equal opportunity.
Children working in the humanities will be likely to confront ideas about
culture and identity, consensus and conflict, about power and the dis-
tribution of resources and opportunities, as a matter of course, not
because their teachers insist upon it, but because those issues are embedded in the material they encounter. This will be true of infants hearing
the tale of Guy Fawkes or trying to agree on systems for classroom
sharing as much as of 10-year-olds learning about nuclear power in the
context of changing forms of energy production.

The humanities, then, will deal with controversy and conflicting
opinion, with ambiguity and uncertainty. The terrain will be far-reaching
and will include the personal, social and political dimensions of human
existence. This is inescapable. These features are what give the humanities their compelling interest and their central importance in a

curriculum that will prepare pupils 'for the opportunities, responsibilities and experiences of adult life' (DES, 1989).

It is the procedures of the humanities that offer protection from the trap of partisanship – open argument, alternative viewpoints, critical reflection, the weighing of evidence, the scrupulous testing and retesting of ideas, the willingness to look across several dimensions of human experience, to triangulate, to double-check a tentative proposition.

The context of the primary school

These features of the humanities fit well with particular aspects of the organization of the primary school, although primary teachers have been less likely to employ conceptions of humanities. 'Topic work' has carried some of the same meaning. For instance, the tradition of integrated humanities work, where the boundaries between subject perspectives are not particularly acknowledged, fits well with an organization of the curriculum through topics, where basic skills are learnt and practised in the interests of a broader investigation: a pedagogy based on supporting active learners, whose ability to give direction to their enquiry fits well with the enquiry-based approaches of history and geography teaching. The notion of doing it 'for real' – reading like real readers (Smith, 1978), writing like writers do (Graves, 1983), engaging in original field work like geographers, asking your own historical questions like historians do – reflects both the general emphasis in primary work, and the newer approaches in the 'disciplines'.

And most importantly, in the primary school, there are the opportunities to take advantage of the structural features of the school – one teacher who knows the children well, long blocks of time, a permanent teaching space equipped like a workshop, flexibly organized and customized for the work in hand, 'owned' by the children and the teacher and used to reflect the work back into the learning process through displays of work, finished and in progress. These features free the teacher to organize with the greatest flexibility, in particular allowing time for practical work in the environment outside the school.

And finally, in the primary school we find an ideology of care for the whole child that does not necessitate personal and social education and pastoral care as bolt-on extras.

In one of its many metamorphoses, 'humanities' is gaining currency in the curriculum language of the primary phase, but this time simply as a shorthand for history and geography, as co-ordination of the implementation of the two sets of National Curriculum Statutory Orders coalesce as a single task, at the level of the LEA, in a cluster of schools, or in the school itself. However there is a general realization that the proposals are not very easily compatible, and that much important work now needs to be done. However, despite the National Curriculum, primary teachers remain well placed to work for a coherent curriculum, where the elements are part of the whole.

History and geography

For better or worse, the humanities have been established in the National Curriculum as history and geography and some benefits accrue from this. There is no doubt that the passionate public debate that has been stimulated by the publication of the proposals for these two subjects has been healthy, in bringing into the professional and public eye some issues of crucial importance. Some version of the debate about the relationship between knowledge and understanding has been aroused by each successive set of subject proposals. Its fiercest expression has been in relation to history, and many commentators have identified this as a struggle over the fundamental aims of education, the ultimate stake-out for a role for education in the transmission of national culture.

Press accounts of the debate have been full of the imagery of military campaigns, and what has seemed to be at stake has been not merely a professional disagreement about the relative importance of process and content, but the role of content in sustaining a particular view. Put simply, the tension has been between a conception of British history as an unproblematic chronological narrative, or as a process of the construction of accounts with different loci, and informed by different perspectives.

Although the Working Group capitulated in the end, so that Attainment Target 1 became 'knowledge and understanding of history', their steadfast, coherent and cogent case, remade at each report stage, and in line with much professional opinion, has made it clear that to have knowledge without understanding would be valueless (Slater, 1991).

First reactions to the publication of the proposals for geography (DES/WO, 1989) celebrated the emphasis on environmental education, but recoiled from the prescriptive catalogue of 'locational knowledge', and the dense array of 'strands' in the Statements of Attainment. By choosing to put content into the Attainment Targets, instead of reserving it for the Programmes of Study, the Geography Working Group signalled its determination to compensate for the perceived failures of geographical education in the recent past. However this 'deficit' view has meant a lost opportunity to use the Attainment Targets for a more ambitious expression of the precise nature of attainment in the subject.

Through the successive stages of the consultation, some sleight of hand has reduced the value of 'place' knowledge, but this is more apparent than real, and more serious still has been the way in which the skills of geographical enquiry have been downgraded in importance, and references to human interests and values filleted out. It seems clear that this has been the result of political interference. Geography, the Working Group suggested, in its proposals, 'also asks the question, "How ought?"' (DES/WO, 1990). The Secretary of State for Education clearly thinks that such inflammatory questions have no place in a geographical education.

However, despite the negative outcomes of these differences, the debate itself gives a higher profile to the issues, and this can have the effect of sharpening our professional thinking and shaping practice in unexpected ways. In this sense, there is at least the possibility that the implementation of a National Curriculum will focus attention on ways of teaching, on identifying the features of good practice and fulfil its aim to ensure development and continuity in children's work, and span age-phase disjunctures. However, the close focus on the minutiae of subject-specific Statements of Attainment is, for the time being, obscuring the need to resolve the destructive competition between core and foundation and the rest. The tension between separate or co-operative development of the curriculum must be resolved in the primary phase by a determined effort to find new models for planning. However, the challenges for the humanities are considerable.

An early prospect is the recognition of a need to widen the knowledge base amongst primary teachers, and not only those concerned with Key Stage 2. It is seductive to believe that the apparent simplicity of what is demanded from teachers of the youngest children requires no major in-service training initiative. We know from HMI that there is no strong tradition of practice in geography and history work (HMI, 1989). The National Monitoring Survey (1982–1986) revealed a dismal picture of uninspiring, predictable work, poor co-ordination, non-existent records of the development of children's understanding and skills over time, and a reliance on old-fashioned information books, work-cards and television series.

Confronted now with the prospect of planning to teach History Study Units with the useful guidance of the now more muted PESC (political, economic, technological and scientific, social and religious, and cultural and aesthetic dimension of history) formula (DES/WO, 1990), teachers will need a broad basis of knowledge and understanding of their own on which to draw in order to teach the deceptively simple Programmes of Study. Little more than a list of items, the Programmes of Study are disarmingly slimline, yet refer to complex concepts. The fuller detail included in the Interim Report (DES/WO, 1990) for the History Study Unit 'Ships and Seafarers', intended only as an example, had many primary teachers reeling at the extent of knowledge implied. This level of detail is missing from the Statutory Orders. And now that we have the welcome inclusion, at the eleventh hour, of some non-European history, the need for resources to be made available for a major in-service training initiative will be even greater.

For geography, the task is different. This is less to do with the nature of the content, much of which is depressingly banal, at least at Key Stage 1, than with the sheer number of disparate items in the Statements of Attainment. Much use is to be made of working with maps, globes, models and from photographs and other representations, and there are particular localities to be chosen for special study. But, all the basic work of researching and gathering resources together for *oneself*, must be accomplished before the work with the children can begin.

Ted Wragg (1991), in his work in Exeter, is showing how primary teachers report their own lack of confidence in science. The danger is that the need for in-service training for the humanities will be eclipsed by those seemingly more pressing needs. Then, in parallel with this need to build confidence in relation to the content of geography and history Programmes of Study, is the more challenging prospect of realizing them in the classroom. In offering History Study Units, the Working Group appears to have outlined some ready-made topics. The approach of the geographers has been quite different. In the case of history, it is important not to assume that the History Study Units are sacrosanct, and cannot be dismantled, reorganized and recombined, both with each other and with elements from the Programmes of Study from other subjects; and in the case of geography, the search must be for some set of organizing principles that will help teachers to find a way through the Programmes of Study that will relate the geography to work in other areas. For instance, teachers wanting to accomplish the History Study Unit on Victorian Britain might choose to include some work on domestic life, families and childhood and also from a school-designed local History Study Unit which would relate to both of those. It is not difficult to see how geographical work on the locality could be incorporated, and opportunities for practising geographical skills would be plentiful.

Alternatively a pair of schools in contrasting localities, working on a project based on a twinning arrangement, might work creatively together to provide each other with rich experiences, both vicarious and first hand, of the space and time dimensions of their home area, exchanging maps, photographs and local resources of all kinds. However, it is relatively easy to identify links of this kind but very much more difficult to generate a plan for the orchestration of the whole.

As schools adapt their forms of topic planning to take account of the National Curriculum, it is clear that a conception of a topic cycle is emerging as a device for planning over a year in the first instance. However, schools that are trying this have been quick to realize the long-term implications. A narrow interpretation of history topics to teach the History Study Units – nine over the four years of Key Stage 2, for instance – will rapidly determine a cycle, fixed or with a few permutations only, that will become a set pattern for a rolling programme for children passing through the junior years. This will be an 'entitlement' of the poorest sort, a lowest common denominator where the best and most creative teaching will be inhibited by the need to keep turning a treadmill of topics believed to 'deliver' National Curriculum Attainment Targets fast enough to fit them all in.

We know clearly how this curriculum has come into being (Lawton and Chitty, 1988) and the teaching profession has had neither the will nor the strategies to deflect it. But we learnt a great deal about the politics of educational decision-making in the 1980s, and perhaps we are no longer so naive. The danger that educational agendas are being set exclusively by the agencies of central Government is now widely perceived and, as teachers move into the phase of implementation, there seems to be a realization that there is no need for such supine deference, and that this next phase of development of the National Curriculum is one in which teachers will reclaim their professional dignity as they join in the process of evaluation and amendment.

From our vantage point as teacher educators, the key questions are to do with the ways in which formal and informal networks of contact between teachers can be created and buttressed, so that we can share and develop classroom work, but working outwards from existing practice. The integration of teachers in training and newly qualified teachers into this process is an important element.

Advice from the National Curriculum Council, new materials from the publishing houses, child-friendly and supportive strategies from other agencies such as museums and galleries, all help to create a climate for professional development, but the thrust must come from school and classroom work. This is not a straightforward process. Accounts of classroom practice, written for publication, or even described in a staffroom seminar, have so much important detail implicit. Where teachers' planning documentation is available, it tells little about the children as individual learners. The development of assessment strategies focuses on the assessment instrument, and on the outcomes for a particular child or group of children, but tells us nothing about the overall planning, or about the teacher's ways of working, or about the whole curriculum. Work on the processes by which children's understanding grows seems to be the most promising line of enquiry, but it is often subject specific, and is in any case, in the humanities, still in its infancy.

New partnerships are being forged as teachers come together for in-service work of different kinds. Schools and LEAs are working more closely with training institutions. There is some prospect that initial training, induction, in-service work, advanced study and research can connect. These initiatives must be grounded in the tradition of action research which aims 'to eliminate the conceptual and institutional boundaries between academic study, research and teaching, and... enhance teachers' capacities and procedures for analysis, appraisal and modification of day-to-day professional ideas and practices' (Alexander, 1984).

Only through these processes, can the National Curriculum, which John Slater has dubbed 'the great hypothesis', be continuously developed and refined by teachers, in the interests of the children.

References

Alexander, R. (1984) *Primary Teaching*. Holt, Rinehart and Winston.

BFI/DES (1989) *Primary Media Education: A Curriculum Statement*. British Film Institute.

Blyth, W. A. L. et al (1976) *Place, Time and Society 8-13*. Collins/ESC.

Blyth, W. A. L. (1990) *Making the Grade for Primary Humanities*. Milton Keynes: Open University Press.

Bruner, J. (1966) *Toward a Theory of Instruction*. Cambridge, Mass: Belknap Press.

Campbell, J. and Little, V. (eds) (1989) *Humanities in the Primary School*. Lewes: The Falmer Press.

DES (1985) *History in the Primary and Secondary Years - an HMI View*. HMSO.

DES (1989) *National Curriculum: From Policy to Practice*. HMSO.

DES/WO (1989) *The National Curriculum Geography Working Group. Interim Report.* HMSO.

DES/WO (1989) *National Curriculum History Working Group: Interim Report.* HMSO.

DES/WO (1990) *National Curriculum History Group. Final Report.* HMSO.

DES/WO (1990) *Geography for Ages 5 to 16.* HMSO.

DES (1991) *Geography in the National Curriculum (England).* HMSO.

DES (1991) *History in the National Curriculum (England).* HMSO.

Dickinson, A. K., Lee, P. J. and Rogers, P. J. (1984) *Learning History.* Heinemann Educational Books.

Graves, D. H. (1983) *Writing: Teachers and Children at Work.* Heinemann Educational Books.

Harlen, W. (1985) 'The question of content.' In: *Teaching and Learning Primary Science.* Harper and Row.

Hicks, D. (1990) 'The World Studies 8-13 Project: A short history.' *Westminster Studies in Education,* Volume 13.

HMI (1989) *The Teaching and Learning of History and Geography* (Aspects of Primary Education series). DES/HMSO.

Inner London Education Authority (1980) *Social Studies in the Primary School.* ILEA.

Kitson Clark, G. (1967) *The Critical Historian.* Heinemann Educational Books.

Lawton, D., Campbell, J. and Burkitt, V. (1971) *Social Studies 8-13.* Schools Council, Evans/Methuen.

Lawton, D. and Chitty, C. (eds) (1988) Bedford Way Papers 33: *The National Curriculum.* London: Institute of Education/Kogan Page.

Proctor, N. (1987) 'History, geography and humanities: A geographer's interpretation.' *Teaching History* 48, 8-12.

Slater, J. (1991) 'History in the National Curriculum: The Final Report of the History Working Group.' In: R. Aldrich (ed.) *History in the National Curriculum.* London: Kogan Page.

Smith, F. (1978) *Reading.* Cambridge: Cambridge University Press.

Taylor, P. H. (1989) In: Campbell, J. and Little, V. (eds) *Humanities in the Primary school.* Lewes: The Falmer Press.

Wragg, E. (1991) 'Outcasts on the Dark Side of Pluto' *Times Educational Supplement.* 15.12.91.

Chapter Six
Art: Understanding, Making and Investigating

Roy Prentice

> This report is written in the conviction that visual education has a crucial role within any curriculum, as relevant to science and technology as it is to the humanities and the social sciences. It is achieved effectively by making, investigating and understanding art. *(National Curriculum Art for Ages 5–14, DES, 1991, p. 1)*

It is the purpose of this chapter to reaffirm the importance of art and design in the National Curriculum, at a time when the curriculum in primary schools is rapidly becoming science and technology led. This marked shift in emphasis demonstrates the extent to which headteachers and teachers have responded to the tremendous pressure exerted by central Government agencies, and local education authorities, to improve the quality of science education through the implementation of the National Curriculum. Within the framework of a subject-based National Curriculum, differentiated types of knowledge are determined as core and foundation subjects. The status attached to individual subjects is reinforced through the order in which they were introduced into schools, the arrangements for their assessment, and the Key Stage at which they cease to be compulsory. A result of this form of organization and presentation of our National Curriculum is that subjects are value laden.

Against this background I shall comment on certain proposals outlined in the Final Report of the National Curriculum Art Working Group and consider some implications for their implementation at Key Stages 1 and 2. In so doing I am mindful of the 'marginal drift' from which art and design education has suffered in many schools, along with the National Curriculum 'overload' with which all primary school teachers are currently trying to cope.

Recommendations of the Art Working Group
The task before the Art Working Group was formidable:

... to advise on a statutory framework which is sufficiently broad and flexible to allow schools wide discretion in relation to the matters to be studied.' *(DES, 1991, p. 71)*

It is to be welcomed that the report encourages a wide range of activity in order that 'the matters to be studied' are seen to represent the subject field more appropriately described as art and design. In the report – which was submitted for consideration by the Art Working Group – members of the Shadow Working Group for art and design in the National Curriculum offer the following working definitions:

> In practice art and design are interdependent and interrelated yet distinguishable activities.
> Artists may be characterised by a concern for making imagery in response to, and to comment on, human experience ...
> Designers may be characterised by a concern for making or improving environments, artefacts and systems.
> *(NSEAD, 1990)*

In general the recommendations contained in the final report have been well received by the majority of art and design educators. The proposed curriculum framework is founded on a strong case for art as a subject in its own right and draws on ideas which have informed the teaching of art and design in schools over the past two decades (Prentice, 1989). A structure for coherent curriculum planning is offered which maximizes opportunities for individual teachers and schools to develop and extend current work in art and design, building on existing strengths and particular interests. Above all it recognizes that art and design can be taught, and can be taught well, by non-specialist primary teachers and secondary specialist teachers alike.

However, the proposed curriculum will make new and considerable demands on a large number of primary teachers and headteachers if the recommended range and depth of work in art and design is to be achieved in all schools. The following position statement reveals the rigour which is required to underpin learning of quality in and through art and design:

> In formulating our recommendations, we have been concerned to give equal attention to the perceptual, contextual and practical aspects of art. Any worthwhile art education involves more than simply making. It is also about observation and the appreciation of the work of others. We consider the processes of art, craft and design to be integrated and holistic. Art cannot be produced in a vacuum but is created within a context, at a particular time

and to fulfil a particular need, be it personal, social, cultural or economic. *(DES, 1991, p. 18)*

An acknowledgement that engagement in art and design activity involves a complex interrelationship between looking, thinking and doing, underpins the proposed structure consisting of the following, equally weighted Attainment Targets:

AT1   *Understanding*
AT2   *Making*
AT3   *Investigating*

It should be stressed that these objectives for an art and design curriculum should be viewed as an organic whole: they do not represent an hierarchical order of importance or a fixed procedural sequence.

Clearly, a reduction from three to two Attainment Targets is favoured by the Secretary of State for Education. If three Attainment Targets are retained, each described by a single word, non-statutory orders will need to provide amplifications to ensure that the subtlety of meanings – the range and complexity of ideas and activities embodied in each word – is fully understood.

During the past 20 years or so, numerous models for art and design education have been devised, and their influences on current practice can be identified. Whilst the terminology differs, a surprisingly high level of agreement exists regarding the value and content of art and design activity. During the past six years, secondary teachers of art and design have gained experience using GCSE criteria as a basis for planning, teaching and evaluating projects. The criteria are made explicit and shared by teachers and students. Many teachers working within the framework of GCSE courses have been influenced by a domain-based approach, in which the conceptual, productive, critical and contextual elements of art and design activity are clearly identified.

The Gulbenkian Foundation Report, *The Arts in Schools* (1982), presented a clearly argued case for the establishment of two vital, interrelated dimensions of an education in the arts, namely participation and appreciation. The National Curriculum Council project bearing the same name, (NCC/SCDC, 1986–89), explored the nature of this interrelationship further using the terms 'making' and 'appraisal'.

In recent years good practice in art and design teaching has been informed by curriculum development in the field of critical and historical studies in art and design, the work of Dyson (1991) and Taylor (1986) being particularly influential. Strategies are used through which children are helped to look at, discuss, understand and evaluate the work of artists, craftspeople and designers from different historical periods and diverse cultural backgrounds. However, the influence of such work can be seen mainly at secondary school level, and the context is, on the whole, fine art orientated.

The report of the Shadow Working Group, published by the National Society for Education in Art and Design (1990), draws attention to key concerns which are central to learning of quality in art and design and which, in various ways, most curriculum models for art and design address. The report expresses these key concerns in terms of four activities: responding, generating ideas, making and evaluating. While the Art Working Group chose not to adopt this model there is much to recommend it. In particular, it offers primary teachers a straightforward, conceptual framework, within which the skills, knowledge and understanding to be acquired and developed through engagement in art and design activity can be identified. Having done so, learning in art and design can be located within an holistic school curriculum. The four activities help teachers to think about, plan and assess work in art and design, using familiar terms which are valid across the curriculum. An approach of this kind can help to demystify art and design in schools whilst revealing, and rigorously reinforcing, the particularity of art and design as a way of knowing, enriched by, and potentially a source of enrichment for, other ways of knowing.

> Implicated in the child's use of art media are understandings which are essentially logico-mathematical, linguistic, spatial and musical. This must not be confused with any tendency to degrade art to a mere servicing tool for other subject areas, but rather to emphasize, for harmonious and interactively efficient teaching through the National Curriculum core and foundation, that the cognitive faculties associated with other forms of learning are intrinsic to the making of art. (*Response to the National Curriculum Art Working Group Interim Report from the Association of Centres for Art and Design Teacher Education, 1991*)

Understanding
'Understanding' is the first Attainment Target.

> Pupils should be able to evaluate and use practically and imaginatively in their own work, the approaches of other artists, craftworkers and designers working in diverse contemporary and historical cultures and context. (*DES, 1991, p. 22*)

I welcome the decision to give such prominence to their concern for the development of understanding. It acknowledges that an understanding of art is necessary to underpin teaching and learning in and through art and design at all levels of schooling. The extent to which teachers' understanding of art is enhanced is reflected in increased opportunities for children to extend their learning through engagement in art and design experience – the mere acquisition of assorted technical skills, and the possession of a facility to reproduce visual imagery, should not be confused with the need for teachers to gain understanding of basic underlying principles, processes and procedures of art and design as a foundation for their work with children. If this Attainment Target is to be properly addressed it will require a major adjustment in the way the subject is perceived in those schools in which art and design activity is merely concerned with making. Teachers and children will need to demonstrate a range of skills, through which works of art, craft and design can be perceived, described, interpreted, evaluated and contextualized. Through the acquisition, refinement and application of a critical language, children can articulate personal responses to the wide range of ideas and feelings embodied in the work of artists, craftspeople and designers who represent different cultural backgrounds, historical periods, ways of working and value systems.

Making

It is likely that the second Attainment Target, 'Making', will be the area in which the majority of primary teachers will feel most confident.

> Pupils should be able to use the skills and knowledge involved in the process of making (including the ability to select and control the use of materials, tools and techniques and an understanding of the visual language of art, craft and design) and apply these in their own work to develop, express and modify their ideas, intentions and feelings. *(DES, 1991, p. 23)*

Where practical work of quality is seen in schools it is more often limited to particular classes, reflecting the interests and values of an individual teacher or group of teachers rather than the outcome of a whole-school policy for art and design. Unfortunately, for some pupils, the experience of making lacks direction and rigour, being confined to the production of artefacts in a cultural vacuum, or the mindless manipulation of materials. When making is reduced to this level, devoid of meaning, it is easy to see how practical activity – which is endorsed by the Art

Working Group as being central to learning in art and design – can be dismissed as an inferior mode of handling ideas.

To make something which has meaning for the maker requires a particular kind of sustained human engagement with ideas and feelings, materials, tools and processes (Gentle, 1990). Making requires skills and knowledge, and demands of the maker an ability to think in terms of qualities and properties of materials, and their impact on intention. This special kind of thinking is described by John Dewey:

> The artist has his problems and thinks as he works. But this thought is more immediately embodied in the object. Because of the comparative remoteness of his end, the scientific worker operates with symbols, words and mathematical signs. The artist does his thinking in the very qualitative media he works in, and the terms lie so close to the object that he is producing that they merge directly into it. *(Dewey, 1979, p. 16)*

It is significant that Professor David Layton (1990) reaffirms the 'privilege of the practical' when discussing technological capability in the context of the National Curriculum. It is this particular kind of thinking, central to making, which provides rich opportunities for art and design activities to contribute to technology programmes in schools.

Investigating
The third Attainment Target is 'Investigating'.

> Pupils should be able to develop their visual perception, recording from direct observation, memory and the imagination and visualize ideas drawing on a wide range of resources which they have selected from the natural and made environment. *(DES, 1991, p. 24)*

Carefully constructed studies made from direct observation of objects, people, environments and events reveal ways in which the language of art and design can be used to record and investigate the world. This approach has been strongly supported by HMI, LEA art and design advisers and teacher educators, and much has been achieved over a period of 20 years. The former ILEA Art and Design Inspectorate was responsible for heightening the visual awareness of a large number of primary teachers through a series of curriculum guidelines and practical INSET workshops. Recording and investigative skills were developed through drawing, and the ways in which art and design can provide starting points for cross-curricular topics were made explicit. As a result, teachers' expectations of what young children are capable of achieving – when provided with and supported by an appropriate framework for learning in art and design – were raised (Rubens and Newland, 1989).

In her refreshingly creative book, *Psychology for Teachers*, Phillida Salmon (1988) reaffirms a view shared by most teachers of young children that 'inquiry is the impetus to understanding'. She goes on to say:

> We construct our world in the interrogations we make of it, the questions we put to it ...it seems that we can develop our understanding only through our own inquiries, we cannot undertake new ventures within the terms of another's initiative.'

We need to have the confidence to trust our sense impressions and ensure that the evidence of our senses is not overruled by predetermined responses. Children need to be helped to look in different ways, rather than to be told what to see. Through their participation in art and design activities children have opportunities to construct and successively re-construct their world view. The visual, tactile, spatial language of art and design is a particularly potent means of interrogating the world, both the private internal world of images, and the shared external world of people, places, objects and events.

Drawing

Drawing is a fundamental form of non-verbal communication and expression, the centrality of which in art and design education, at all levels, is acknowledged by the Art Working Group. It is the intention that the importance of drawing should be restated and its diverse functions understood as a basis for work undertaken with children from their earliest years of schooling. Drawing needs to be harnessed as a powerful tool for learning across the curriculum, establishing sound practice beginning with nursery and reception classes. All children draw unaided before they develop sophisticated communication systems using spoken and written language. All schools employ graphic means to support learning in a variety of subjects.

> Whenever there is a need to record or express ideas which cannot be done effectively with words, numbers or gestures, graphic means such as diagrams, sketches, plans and notation systems may be used instead, all of which depend on the basic skill of drawing. *(DES, 1991, p. 55)*

Unfortunately, many adults, including teachers, have a narrow concept of drawing, both in what the activity entails and what the outcome should look like. When drawing is limited to copying, making photographic likenesses of things observed, it is hardly surprising that most people experience a reinforcement of their inability to draw. This situation, in turn, reduces the confidence of many primary teachers when encouraged to use drawings as a means of promoting learning across the curriculum.

An important purpose of the National Curriculum for art is to make the different functions of drawing explicit, and promote an extended concept of drawing which fosters a wide range of possibilities through two-dimensional and three-dimensional investigations and responses. Drawing can be used to analyse, investigate and record closely observed elements of the natural and manufactured world. Through the act of drawing, looking becomes more sharply focused, and engagement with the focus of attention is sustained. Information gathered is modified in the light of further inquiry. The work evolves as graphic equivalents are invented, relationships between parts are clarified and insights are deepened. Through drawing, a special kind of intimacy develops between the person engaged in the activity, the focus of attention and the chosen expressive media.

Drawing is an 'outward looking search process' but it is also an 'inward looking retrieval system' (Art Advisers Association, 1979). Equally important is the opportunity which drawing offers for highly personal images, often of indeterminate origin, to be dredged up from a private world of the imagination, dreams, fantasy, memory, associations, to be explored through being externalized, and to be viewed afresh, combined and better understood, as a result of being shared with others.

In the process of making a drawing, questions are posed and possibilities emerge as new ideas are generated through the dialogue which occurs between idea and media. When viewed in this way teachers and children are able to relate their involvement in drawing to the ways in which drawing is, and has been, regarded by established artists. Drawing occupied a central position in Henry Moore's work throughout his long career. He referred to it as 'a means of keeping pace with a fertile imagination'. His further elaboration reveals some of the different functions which drawing fulfils, particularly in relation to making connections between two-dimensional and three-dimensional modes of working.

My drawings are done mainly as a help towards making sculpture – as a means of generating ideas for sculpture, tapping oneself for the initial idea, and as a way of sorting out ideas and developing them. ... And I use drawings as a method of study and observation of natural form (drawings from life, drawings of bones, shells, etc) ...And I sometimes draw just for its own enjoyment. *(Henry Moore, quoted in Ghiselin, 1952)*

From an early age children should be aware of different kinds of drawing systems, including computer-generated images, together with the criteria which determine the forms they take. An architect's plan, a map, a book illustration, a Calder mobile and a pastel drawing by Degas have different functions; they are made and need to be 'read' in different ways.

Three-dimensional design

Traditionally, few primary schools have developed a systematic approach to three-dimensional work in art and design. In nursery and reception classes junk modelling – the random sticking together of found objects, mainly commercial packaging – provides experience of resistant materials whilst dough, plasticine and clay offer parallel experiences of plastic materials. Frequently such activities lack challenge and fail to identify technical skills and concepts through carefully structured, increasingly rigorous tactile experiences, which should provide a basis for extending work at Key Stage 2. Currently, where inventive three-dimensional work of quality is undertaken at Key Stage 2, it often forms a part of topic work, in which the full potential of the art and design content remains untapped.

Given the requirement that art and design should make a distinctive contribution to the teaching of design and technology in the National Curriculum, a refreshing new context exists, within which three-dimensional work has a major part to play. At present the most common approach to three-dimensional studies in art and design in primary schools reinforces a skills-based rationale, which reflects a craft-based tradition, through which materials and processes have become associated with prescribed outcomes. With the introduction into the school curriculum of a new subject, technology, there exists an exciting opportunity for primary teachers to help define it, the values it embodies, its content and the directions in which it could develop. A re-examination of the nature and range of three-dimensional work in art and design should be an important part of this process. Without the territorial claims of specialist departments and the timetable constraints of secondary schools, primary teachers can use their greater fluidity to achieve imaginative cross-curricular connections between art and design, and design and technology. It is necessary to reconsider the basis on which materials are selected, organized, used, combined and valued, if attitudes towards three-dimensional activities in art and design are to change. Young infants develop an intelligence of feeling through direct bodily contact with diverse surfaces and through manipulation of a range of substances and objects. Learning through sensory experience is equally highly valued by nursery and reception class teachers and specialist teachers of art and design. Playing with sand, clay, water, helps to develop a sense of weight, balance, softness, warmth, coolness, moistness as well as curved and angular forms and movements. The creative process in art and design involves a period when the maker becomes acquainted with the qualities and potential of expressive media through playing with materials.

Historical, critical and contextual studies
In recent years a major influence on art and design education in secondary schools has been the introduction of an historical, critical and contextual studies dimension to practical courses, particularly at GCSE level. Personal responses through making are enriched and extended through a deeper understanding of the work of other artists, craftspeople and designers. The interim report for art points out in its introduction that:

> Pupils need to learn that pictures and symbols can have several meanings,
> and that different interpretations of them are possible and valid in a modern
> industrial society and multicultural world. *(DES, 1991, p 1)*

However, at secondary level, in many schools, historical and critical studies remain fine art orientated and, to a large extent, are dominated by a western European tradition. The same criticism has been voiced about examples which appear in the report. Clearly, there is an urgent need for historical, critical and contextual studies in art and design education to embrace the work of ethnic artists, women artists, and designers.

From an early age primary school children should be initiated into the work of other artists, craftspeople and designers. Through language, teachers can focus their looking and develop and refine descriptive and interpretative skills. Visual resources of quality are essential. Good use can be made in the classroom of secondary resources – reproductions, postcards, slides, videos – to support more ambitious work derived from visits to museums and galleries and artists in residence schemes.

The introduction of a National Curriculum for art has far-reaching implications for the initial and in-service education and training of teachers. In particular, primary teachers – many of whom discontinued their own education in art and design at the age of 13 or 14 – will require support and guidance if they are to develop sufficiently in confidence and competence to implement a whole-school policy for art and design which meets National Curriculum criteria. Schools will need to identify more clearly the expectations of a subject co-ordinator for art and design and primary PGCE and BEd courses, along with local authority advisory services, will need to include staff with expertise in art and design education firmly located in a context of primary practice.

It is necessary to make explicit different ways in which art and design offer rich starting points for cross-curricular projects to ensure that art and design experiences are dovetailed into existing Programmes of Study, topic and thematic work. Unless this is achieved through a genuine understanding of the particular contributions to learning which art and design makes within a curriculum conceived as a coherent whole, the full potential of art and design is likely to remain unrealized. Similarly the basic concepts and skills which PGCE and BEd students acquire in their initial training courses, through an all too brief acquaintanceship with art and design education, should provide the starting points for systematic development through INSET opportunities (Sharp, 1990).

It is heartening to witness the extent to which students following a one-year primary PGCE course at the Institute of Education, London University, are able to demonstrate understandings and skills in art and design, following a 15-hour workshop. Students engage in art and design activity at their own level, in order to experience, from the inside, how ideas emerge, grow and require support over a period of time. In so doing they become increasingly aware of the conditions which they, as teachers, will need to create in their classrooms, to maximize learning in and through art and design.

In this short chapter I have drawn attention to three important areas of art and design education; drawing, three-dimensional studies and historical, critical and contextual studies. By focusing on each of these areas in relation to Attainment Targets, within PGCE, BEd and INSET courses, I believe much could be achieved to improve the quality and extend the range of art and design activity at Key Stages 1 and 2. In so doing, the importance of art and design in the primary school curriculum would be reaffirmed by teachers through their day-to-day practice. After all, primary teachers have the responsibility for the quality of six, a total of nine, years of compulsory education in art and design.

Art is profoundly important for the full growth of the individual because it deals with ideas, feelings and experiences visually and develops a language of visual, tactile and spatial responses which create and sustain images. To develop an intelligence about visual matters is not a haphazard affair any more than it is with other languages. Experiences of looking and interpreting, analysing and solving problems, visualizing and finding appropriate forms and images for our feelings and ideas are all capable of refinement and enrichment through teaching. *(Gentle, 1985, p. 96)*

References

Art Advisers Association (1979) *Learning Through Drawing.*

Association of Centres for Art and Design Teacher Education (1991) *Report to the National Curriculum Art Working Group.*

DES (1991) *National Curriculum Art for Ages 5–14.* HMSO.

Dewey, J. (1934) *Art as Experience.* Paragon Books (1979).

Dyson, A. (1991) *Empathy and Art Education.* Birmingham Polytechnic: The Article Press.

Gentle, K. (1985) *Children and Art Teaching.* Croom Helm.

Gentle, K. (1990) 'Art Making for Individuals.' In: *Journal of Art and Design Education,* Vol 9, No 3.

Gulbenkian Report (1982, revised edition 1989) *The Arts in Schools.* Gulbenkian Foundation.

Henry Moore, quoted in Ghiselin, B. (1952) *The Creative Process.* Mentor.

Layton, D. (1990) *Technology Audit for Institute of Education, University of London.* (Unpublished paper).

National Curriculum Council Project (1986–1989) *The Arts in Schools.*

NSEAD (The National Society for Education in Art and Design) (1990) *Report of the Shadow Working Group for Art and Design in the National Curriculum.*

Prentice, R. (1989) 'Some Recent Influences and Directions.' In: Dyson, A. (ed.) *Looking, Making and Learning.* (Bedford Way Series). London: Kogan Page.

Rubens, M. and Newland, M. (1989) *A Tool for Learning: Some Functions of Art in Primary Education.* Direct Experience.

Salmon, P. (1988) *Psychology for Teachers: An Alternative Approach.* Hutchinson.

Sharp, C. (1990) *Developing the Arts in Primary Schools: Good Practice in Teacher Education.* National Foundation for Educational Research.

Taylor, R. (1986) *Educating for Art.* Longmans.

Chapter Seven
Physical Education

Janet Sparkes and Barry Fry

The arrival of the Physical Education National Curriculum Document needs to be viewed in the context of the 1988 Education Reform Act, which recommended the establishment of a National Curriculum comprising core and foundation subjects. Physical education was identified in the legislation as a foundation subject, thus ensuring its place in the curriculum of all 5- to 16-year-olds.

The details contained within the physical education proposals are the result of intensive discourse over a ten-month period by an appointed Working Group, which had the task of advising the Secretaries of State on appropriate Attainment Targets and Programmes of Study for physical education. The group worked within constraints imposed by specific terms of reference, the most significant being the requirement to provide a framework for working which was:

> ...sufficiently broad and flexible to allow schools wide discretion in relation to the matters to be studied. *(DES, 1991, Annex B, para. 2)*[1]

The lack of prescription in this requirement differs from that imposed on other subjects and could be viewed favourably as regards the freedom it gives schools and teachers delivering the curriculum. However, of greater significance may be the constraints emanating from the proposal by the Secretaries of State that only one Attainment Target should be included in the Order, with statutory End of Key Stage Statements. The Working Group was also asked to make recommendations for non-statutory Statements of Attainment calibrated into ten levels.

---

1   All subsequent references are to this publication.

Although the terms of reference may have been inhibiting, a major strength of the proposal lies in the insight it gives into the nature of physical education. Teachers are encouraged to spend time digesting the essence of the rationale, drawing out the key concepts in the Programmes of Study, reflecting on the challenges presented to practice in the sections related to special needs and equal opportunities, and examining delivery in relation to cross-curricular matters. This process will help the teacher capture something of the significance of the proposal and become more reflective in considering what physical education 'is' and what physical education 'does'.

Taken as a whole, the proposal helps the teacher reflect on practice (process) as well as outcomes (product). Possible misconceptions of physical education are challenged in an overall statement which encourages consideration of the physical education curriculum in terms of a process which ensures that the needs of all children, of all abilities, and from differing social and cultural backgrounds, are met. A principal feature underpinning the whole thesis of the proposal is the concept of entitlement through considered, caring pedagogy.

Against this background it is necessary to engage in a more critical assessment of the physical education proposal as it applies to teachers in primary schools. Any discussion concerning implementation inevitably centres on two interrelated, fundamental issues – the consideration of ends and means; or the identification of appropriate aims and objectives and the resources needed for effective delivery. In one sense the proposal for physical education exemplifies a statement of intent, but it is important to recognize the statutory binding requirements of the proposal and statements which are recommendations or non-statutory requirements. The manner in which schools and teachers attend to these statements may have serious implications for the quality of teaching and learning.

What follows is a discussion of the underlying rationale and the structure of the proposal, in terms of the statutory and non-statutory requirements, and the implications of these for schools and teachers, and then a more general review of broader issues concerning delivery and implementation.

End of Key Stage Statements

Within the terms of reference, the Working Group was asked to recommend one short and general Statement of Attainment that relates to each Key Stage as a whole. Along with art and music, physical education is not expected to give an attainment level for each child. The minimum statutory requirement for reporting on pupils' achievements is based on these End of Key Stage Statements.

No valid educational reasons have been given by the Secretaries of State as to why physical education, art and music have only End of Key Stage statutory requirements. Inevitably, this lack of statutory stringency might undermine physical education's true worth and compromise its status and placement on the curriculum.

We consider these End of Key Stage Statements to be simplistic, not reflecting realistically the diversity and essence of physical education. Such a limited approach could seriously reduce the quality of any assessment and reporting of pupil achievement. It is difficult to see how realistic expectations of pupil achievement can be satisfied across the range of pupil ability in one generalized statement.

However, it is important to reaffirm one major principle embodied within the ideology of the whole proposal – that of entitlement. Children of all abilities are entitled to have access and opportunity within the National Curriculum. The proposal for physical education, with its generalized End of Key Stage Statements, enables teachers to make modifications and adaptations in content and delivery, thus accommodating children with wide and varied educational needs.

Although the intention of the Working Group to present statements that require little or wide interpretation is recognized, in achieving this, a detail which would give greater clarity to these statements may have been lost. Open to wide interpretation, without clear criteria, the End of Key Stage Statements are in danger of losing credibility.

Children of all abilities could conceivably satisfy and be accommodated within these imprecise Statements of Achievement. Extending, motivating and challenging both children and teachers to improve performance may be unreliable. In other words, the End of Key Stage Statements are not sufficiently differentiated or demanding and could lead to the acceptance by teachers of mediocre performance of pupils, not giving sufficient credit to gifted and talented children, and may be unrealistic in assessing weaker performance.

Non-statutory Levels of Attainment

Although we may not have a great deal of confidence in the statutory End of Key Stage Statements, it is reassuring to recognize the pedagogical worth of the non-statutory Levels of Attainment. The essence of physical education, as reflected through the teaching and learning process, is realized within these non-statutory levels. They bear out the process and product of pupil achievement and allow for greater differentiation. They reflect elements of pupil learning expressed through knowledge, skills and understanding which are inextricably embraced within the process of planning, performing and evaluating. This ongoing, cyclical process by children of continual review, modification and adaptation is an essential feature of all teaching and should help consolidate a common, coherent approach to learning and teaching across the curriculum. These non-statutory Levels of Attainment are thus essential to teachers for interpreting Key Stage requirements and planning for cohesion and progression.

This necessarily will involve teachers in appraising their teaching. These non-statutory Levels of Attainment reflect the nature of the learning experience: children develop, explore, practise, adapt, select, improve, refine, assess and apply. These actions convey not only the process by which children learn, but also the process by which teachers teach, a process which is encapsulated in the notion of children's 'doing' and 'thinking'. There may still be schools where product-focused, nonreflective, habitual practice still occurs. For teachers in such schools, the proposals for physical education may be more challenging.

Programmes of Study
Since the End of Key Stage Statements are general and imprecise, it is important to have more precise Programmes of Study – they need to exemplify good practice. In this regard, the Programmes of Study offer a very credible basis for practice. Teachers in primary schools will see the Programmes of Study as important features. They will look to them for guidance in matters of curriculum balance, continuity and progression.

For Key Stages 1 and 2, curriculum balance is suggested through six areas of activity – athletics, dance, games, gymnastics, outdoor and adventurous activities, and swimming, with an emphasis placed on gymnastics, dance and games. Schools will have the flexibility to choose whether they teach swimming during Key Stage 1 or 2, or across both.

In relation to these different activities, assimilating the Rationale for Programmes of Study (Appendix D) is to be recommended. Although something of the distinctiveness of each movement area is captured in the earlier sections of the proposal – for example, exploring moods and feelings (Dance, Key Stage 1), playing games with simple rules (Games, Key Stage 1), learning the principles of water safety (Swimming, Key Stages 1 and 2) – a clearer picture of what are the central features of each activity is best obtained from reading this more detailed section. Here, the teacher is presented with a use of language which is more precise than that found in the earlier sections. This is particularly the case in relation to dance and is to be welcomed. The more detailed rationale for dance contributes significantly to identifying the unique contribution that dance can make within the physical education curriculum. However, the links between dance and other areas of the curriculum could be more explicitly stated, encouraging and fostering collaborative teaching.

Programmes of Study are particularly helpful in presenting to teachers a framework which considers progression and balance within the curriculum. They contain statutory requirements expressed through the six areas of activity, supported by non-statutory recommendations, and in this respect offer schools a degree of flexibility in terms of curriculum implementation.

Although it is accepted that a proposal which is too prescriptive could lead to a product/content orientated curriculum, a more open-ended programme does not necessarily support the intention to obtain curriculum balance. Six areas of activity are to be welcomed and are helpful in understanding the context of physical education, although it would have been more helpful if the Working Party could have been more specific in advising teachers and schools on matters of curriculum balance across and within all six areas of activity.

The Programmes of Study provide a basis on which schools and teachers can develop a scheme of work. However, at the risk of being too technocratic, teachers in primary schools will need help and assistance in articulating developmentally sound, progressive and appropriately challenging content. Equally, teachers, through their schemes and presentational method, will need to demonstrate how children of all abilities can be given purposeful learning opportunities.

Again, as with the central ethic of entitlement, the fundamental principle of access and opportunity figures prominently within the structure of the Programmes of Study. They are not so prescriptive that children with special educational needs could not be accommodated. It is not the context or content of the Programmes of Study which might limit or restrict inclusion for all children, but the selection by teachers of inappropriate teaching strategies and methods. Indeed, explicit reference is made in the proposal (Chapter 6 and Appendix A) to matters concerning equal opportunity and a set of guiding principles is presented for teachers concerning issues relating to entitlement, access, opportunity and integration. The proposal challenges teachers with long held beliefs, prejudices and stereotypical attitudes to reappraise their teaching of physical education in terms of 'what' is taught and 'how' it is presented to children.

An examination in this regard will be necessary in considering, as the proposal says, pupil responses to femininity, masculinity and sexuality, to the whole range of ability and disability, from gifted and talented to those with disability and handicap, to ethnic, social and cultural diversity, and the ways in which all of these relate to children in physical education.

The Working Group has considered these issues very well and must be congratulated on the way in which children of all abilities and from differing backgrounds could be accommodated within physical education. The lack of prescription within the Programmes of Study should allow teachers sufficient scope and flexibility in exercising their professional judgement to set appropriate attainable tasks, choosing suitable teaching methods and thus enabling them to provide positive, rewarding and meaningful experiences for all children.

Cross-curricular implications

Although, for Key Stages 1 and 2, the Programmes of Study present physical education as embracing six areas of activity, the Working Group acknowledges the eclectic nature and place of physical education within the context of the whole school curriculum. In particular, the intrinsic and instrumental worth of physical education in fostering and developing cross-curricular matters is recognized, especially in cultivating cross curricular skills and themes (Chapter 11 and Appendix B).

Again this has significant implications on how teachers teach and the strategies they engage. It is difficult to see how a teacher-driven, didactic approach could develop in children the cross-curricular skills of problem solving. Indeed, a particular feature of the Attainment Target of physical education, explicitly affirmed both in the Programmes of Study and the non-statutory Levels of Attainment, is the process of planning, performing and evaluating, involving children in the actions of observing, describing and analysing. In this regard, the cross-curricular skills of communicating, of speaking and listening, agreeing and disagreeing are essential features of all teaching in physical education.

Perhaps more recognizable within the context of physical education are the cross-curricular themes of health education and personal and social education. However, the beneficial effects of exercise and the associated aspects of fitness, hygiene and diet are not presented as discrete components within the Programmes of Study, but are seen as interwoven issues. In the same way, the place of personal and social education permeates the whole fabric of physical education.

Broader resource implications

One issue which is not addressed in the proposal is the amount of curriculum time which should be devoted to physical education. Indeed, the Secretaries of State insisted that this should not concern the Working Group and that the issue of curriculum placement should be left to individual schools. Since physical education is one of the last foundation subjects to be addressed, it is possible that some schools may squeeze and marginalize its place in the curriculum.

The Programmes of Study propose that six areas of activity should be included in the Order. Although no statutory proposal is presented concerning the amount of curriculum time that should be devoted to each area, it is patently obvious that if schools consider the requirements of these Programmes of Study in terms of balance and breadth, adequate time must be made available.

Inevitably, the Programmes of Study may necessitate a considerable influx of basic material resources – making available, bats, sticks, balls of various shapes and sizes, mats, etc. However, the most important factor concerning the successful delivery of the physical education curriculum is the enthusiasm, commitment and skill of the teacher. This has serious implications for initial teacher training and INSET provision. With no desired statement of intent, no effective means of implementation is possible without the full co-operation and engagement of colleges, LEAs, schools and teachers. This will involve a number of positive responses.

The Programmes of Study and non-statutory Levels of Attainment illustrate what teachers should expect in terms of outcomes and in this sense have more significance for *assessment* of pupil achievement (see' Chapter 10 of the proposal). There are named physical skills, for example, running, jumping, travelling, turning, twisting, rolling, balancing, swinging and climbing; there are identifiable physical attributes which include developing control, co-ordination and poise; there are identifiable behaviours, for instance, co-operating, responding, listening and working within rules; there are expectations in relation to cognitive skills, illustrated by planning, describing, explaining, composing and applying; and there are identifiable processes and outcomes related to health issues, to aesthetic development of children and to personal and social education.

Many of the above points serve to illustrate the feeling of balance that pervades the proposal. Teachers are encouraged to look at the document with the following in mind: the balance suggested in teaching styles; the balance between technical and creative experiences; the balance in the social demands made of the child – working individually, with a partner, in a group, co-operatively and competitively; and the balance between contexts in which activity takes place – athletics, games, gymnastics, dance, swimming and outdoor and adventurous activities.

In other words, teachers will have to review the manner in which they teach. Effective delivery will involve greater knowledge and under-standing of subject content (progression and lead-up activities), greater understanding about catering for children of all abilities, appropriateness of matching tasks to different children, and a realization of effective methodology, using appropriate teaching styles and strategies. All these issues are vital in ensuring that pupils are provided with the opportunity to appraise and evaluate their work as an integral part of the learning process, enabling them to become active learners. This can only be achieved through the explicitly planned and rational actions of teachers, thus offering children greater opportunity to learn beyond the mere art of doing.

Conclusions

In keeping with the emphasis in the National Curriculum documentation in general, the physical education proposal places emphasis on the concepts of breadth, balance, relevance and differentiation. This is to be welcomed, as is the spirit of the whole document. The principles and practices expounded are rooted in good primary practice. The enthusiastic, committed and imaginative application of these ideas should foster a programme of physical education in our schools which challenges the abilities and meets the needs of all children.

References
DES (1991) *Final Report of the Working Party: Physical Education for Ages 5–16.* HMSO.

Chapter Eight
Music: Releasing the Musician Within

June Boyce-Tillman

For the last 25 years, in various parts of the country, people have been pushing back the frontiers of music education, to expand the boundaries of a subject once regarded as the most elitist and least useful in the school curriculum. The second paragraph of a letter from Sir John Mandell, Chair of the Music Working Group, summarizes the philosophy behind many of these workers:

> Our aim has been to design a programme of music education which is accessible to all pupils, whatever their abilities and level of maturity, and one which can be easily understood by parents, governors and teachers.

Three Attainment Targets

The structure of the Attainment Targets suggested reflects the analytical practice that many of us have already been using to provide a balanced curriculum. It was drawn initially from Swanwick (1979). These targets are now entitled 'performing', 'composing' and 'appraising' and are, in general, clearly differentiated, although a muddle over movement to music, which rightly belongs under audience listening, left it subsumed under Appraising. Under the heading 'performing' is included singing and playing instruments, performing music in a variety of styles, to wide audiences, and some understanding of symbols (not necessarily western European classical notation).

'Composing' includes a number of activities that gained popularity initially in the 1960s – sound exploration, improvising, arranging and more polished original pieces at the higher Levels of Attainment. The End of Key Stage Statements require pupils both to compose and also retain their work in some way, on tape or in symbolic form. In the End of Key Stage Statements it is a pity that the phase in which children are interested in exploring the expressive character of music is not referred to (although it is present in the Programmes of Study), as this is an important stage in children's musical development. This is the time when they are taken up with the representation of mood and image in music, allying both their songs and instrumental pieces with poetry, dance and drama. It is one phase clearly recognized by specialist and generalist teachers.

'Appraising' is a term which many people will find unfamiliar in a musical context. It represents a sharpening of the Interim Report which had two distinct Attainment Targets entitled 'listening' and 'knowing'. Listening has always been a confusing term in relation to the music curriculum without qualification, as, in one sense, no musical activity is possible without it. Swanwick's original term, 'audition', was an attempt to overcome this problem, and in many places now this has been replaced by the term 'audience-listening' as a less-loaded term to represent what Swanwick called 'responsive listening *as*, although not necessarily *in*, an audience'. It is in many ways the most difficult of the forms of musical engagement to assess, for it often shows few outward manifestations. These always use another medium, like movement, words or graphic representation and so depend on a grasp of another medium for assessment. In the new term, movement is specified along with discussion, which is essential for valid work exploring this area with young children, especially as they are required to examine their 'own aesthetic response'. There is the inclusion of information about music, 'its historical and cultural background', with a requirement that this be of 'different genres and styles'. Yet the linking of these aspects together should prevent any attempt to return to sterile music lessons consisting of note-taking on the lives of 'great composers' (sometimes without a note of their music being heard) or counting the number of keys on a flute without the pupils being able to distinguish the sound of the flute from that of a trumpet.

And so a model now well established in the world of music education will be the basis of INSET courses on this document, exploring, refining and sharpening it. In the interests of precision they are rightly Profile Components, for they are such as defined in the original TGAT document. But earlier reports had already confused these terms and the Working Party has rightly gone with the now established usage. Profile Component as a term has in the Final Document rightly been discarded.

The joy of these three Attainment Targets is that they establish music as an essentially practical subject in which everyone is capable of practical participation. Concentration on the purely theoretical has been the prime way of excluding people from its hallowed territory. Inside everyone there is a musician waiting to be released; no longer can we be content with a map of musical ability which excludes some people by an accident of birth. If the National Curriculum means anything, it means music for everyone and must start from the basic assumption that *everyone* is musical. With that assumption must come a map of music education that does encompass everyone – the 'groaners', the unco-ordinated, those whose musical fulfilment will be in styles other than the western European classical tradition and so on.

The Secretary of State has problems with this, largely because of the resource implications which are listed in order of priority as teacher supply and training, initial teacher training, equipment, accommodation, music support services and use of time. It is good to see that classroom-based INSET is encouraged and that this should be followed by longer term support by music consultants (essential with the present recommendations at the top of the primary school), either from the school staff or an outside agency. It is a pity that the provision of smaller, sound-proofed rooms is linked with 'group work in secondary schools'. Anyone who has attempted to do any of the activities outlined in this document in an open-plan primary school will be aware of the problems presented by our present primary school architecture. But in other respects, I hope that this list is the basis of resourcing and funding for the years ahead.

At the time of writing this chapter the Secretary of State is still asking for a reduction of the three Attainment Targets to two or one. I trust that there will be sufficient response in favour of the structure as set out in this document to retain all three. Not only are they well established in the world of INSET, but also such so-called 'simplification' will almost certainly result in a greater confusion of thought and perception. 'Making music' will not do to encompass composing and performing. Although these two areas are not separate in many cultures, composing is not long enough established in the curriculum to hold its own under an Attainment Target entitled making music. If it were to disappear, we should lose an area that has brought a whole new dimension to the curriculum, not only because it has proved accessible to generalist primary teachers who find the problem-solving techniques learnt in other curriculum areas useful here, but also because it has brought a new criterion into the area of musical choice – that of 'do I like it, or don't I?' That is not to say that this is the criterion for assessment, a process that will be a topic for many future discussions, but it is an area where freedom to experiment is valued, where even adults can 'play' freely, where what appears initially to be a mistake can be the best idea you ever had, and choices can be made on the basis of personal taste rather than in the tighter confines of performing in which, for example, if Mozart wrote F# you have no choice as to what to play. Again this limited concept of 'rightness' and 'wrongness' has limited people's access to the subject (to which many 'failed' piano pupils will testify).

I am already using these categories in initial training of generalist students. I find them, after clear explanation, easily understood and readily usable in analysing the musical processes involved in any musical activity. We play, for example, a game like 'Magic Drum' in which a drum is passed round while this rhyme is recited: 'Magic drum, magic drum, what sounds can you make?' Whoever has the drum when the rhyme stops improvises freely on the drum. The students are able easily to see that this activity encompasses both composing and performing. If we discuss the nature of the musical offering within the group we are then adding appraising. When we are singing a song by someone else, as we might in an assembly, we are only engaged in performing. This is clearly a serviceable tool.

But the example of the Magic Drum game also shows how the structure is an analytical tool, not an organizational guide for lessons. It is particularly important in primary schools that the activities of performing, composing and appraising should be interwoven in lesson plans for they each serve to 'reinforce and develop learning and skill in the others'. Treated flexibly rather than as prescriptive and limiting, I do not think that there is anything of value that has been going on in our primary school music curriculum that will not be permitted under the terms of this document. I hope that people will use it imaginatively.

Programmes of Study
The Programmes of Study give a great deal of scope for both personal and institutional variety: the layout is now clear and there are helpful suggestions for fulfilling the demands. In each Programme of Study there are three sections. The first starts: 'Children should be taught how to...'; the second begins: 'Children should be given opportunities to....'; and the third opens with: 'Children should be encouraged to...'. These clearly represent different strategies for different aspects of the experience. For Key Stage 1 they are to be taught how to:

> Listen attentively to their own and others' music, in order to recognize and, using simple musical vocabulary, make broad distinctions within the main musical elements of:
> *pitch*   high/low
> *duration*   pulse; rhythm; long/short sounds

pace   fast/slow
timbre   quality of sound
texture   one sound/several sounds
dynamics   loud/quiet
structure pattern; phrasing; repetition/contrast
silence

But they should be given opportunities to:

> ...explore, select and use a range of sound sources including their voices, their bodies, sounds from the environment and appropriate instruments, tuned and untuned, and discuss their properties, eg *have access to a 'music corner' and explore the sounds the voice can make.*

This division identifies clearly the two poles that need to be passed on by direct teaching and things which can best be discovered in free exploration. The music exploration so important in the infant classroom can now almost be regarded as statutory and all youngsters will be able to go there and indulge in the free exploration of tone, colour and pulse so vital to their musical development. Under the heading 'encouraged to' comes the sharing of activities that they do in their own time like:

> ...relate musical activities undertaken in their own time to work done in class, *eg talk about songs sung with parents and grandparents.*

It is a pity that only in the Programme of Study for Key Stage 4 are the links with the three strands of performing, composing and appraising clearly made. This would have been helpful throughout the proposal, particularly for generalist primary teachers. On the other hand it does emphasize the need for the holistic delivery of the music curriculum. For example, in the Key Stage 2 Programme of Study it is recommended that children:

> ...develop musical ideas through improvising, composing and arranging, responding to a range of stimuli and using appropriate musical structures, *eg create a piece in response to a rhythmic pattern, movement, drama, a series of pictures, others' compositions, first-hand experience...; improvise a vocal 'verse' to alternate with a given 'chorus'.*

An example of this is the creation in groups of a piece using the pattern of a small motif that recurs. For instance, if A is a tune on a xylophone between contrasted sections on other instruments (which we can call sections B, C and D), the group could devise the musical pattern such as ABACADA. Each group plays its piece to the others: the audience is asked to identify how the contrast is achieved. Is it, for example, by the use of different instruments, or by having a different rhythm, or a different volume level or expressive character, or a different tune? Is it successful in achieving contrast between sections? On the basis of these comments the groups go back to refine their compositions. In this lesson or series of lessons all three areas – composing, performing and appraising – have been embraced, the appraising leading back to composing which may lead to a repeat of a cycle that resembles one often only accessible to established composers in the past.

With INSET back-up, these Programmes of Study can prove very helpful to generalist teachers. Perhaps one of the most important ways initially is in proving that they have been doing a great deal of it already, for example teaching children how to:

> ...listen to music of a widening variety of styles, times and cultures, covering a wide range of moods and purposes, and acquire some basic knowledge and understanding of its social, historical and cultural background.

Music and the generalist primary teacher

This confirmation of existing good practice is essential if the 'music for all' philosophy behind this document is to be implemented. Although the document reflects the developments that have been going on for the last 25 years, these have been happening in a somewhat piecemeal way across the country, and many primary schools in particular have been content to marginalize or ignore music if there was no one who felt able to teach it, or thought that four children learning the guitar could pass for a music curriculum for the whole school. Those days are over, but in our primary schools we have teachers who are, in general, the products of an older system than that set out here – a system that for many of them generated only a sense of failure. It is often more the spirit in which the experience is given that communicates itself more strongly to the pupils than the knowledge itself; it is important that the generalist teachers are sufficiently empowered and enabled to pass on a sense of confidence rather than their own fear.

It is often in the area of singing that this sense of failure was initially set up. The assertion that 'I am not musical' or 'I am tone deaf' can usually be traced back to a primary school experience in which the person was asked to open their mouth and let no sound come out or, worse still, was forcibly ejected from a singing situation. There is only one way, in my experience, in which a person will never learn to sing in tune with others and that is by stopping them singing. That is, paradoxically, the way that singing has been 'taught' to many of our generalist primary teachers. The map of singing that was in use in our schools was too small. A 'school singing style' developed that was a watered down version of cathedral choir boys. Singing is everyone's birthright (like speech) but, in order to realize this, the map of singing as presented in our schools, must include other singing styles, other vocal tone colours and, especially, low pitches. Many people whose most favoured note was low (lower than the G above middle C or even middle C itself), found no songs in school that they could even approach. The pitching of songs for young singers between G and D (appropriate for the only young voices of which the musical experts had experience, ie cathedral choir boys) was not appropriate for a 'music for all' curriculum, and in its operation we lost many of our best potential altos. We have to correct the legacy of the past, as well as establishing a new singing regime that will enable all children to realize their potential. The general introduction to the End of Key Stage Statements on performing starts:

> Pupils should develop the skills and competencies needed to perform, through singing (including a wide variety of sound-making with the voice) and playing instruments, their own compositions and those of others in a variety of styles.

What a refreshing attempt to redeem the past! The 'demusicalized' teachers need to return, with their pupils, to the infinite range of sounds possible with the human voice, and traditionally explored in early years in songs and poems involving animal noises, in order to rediscover their own singing tone and note and, from the exploration of these, their own capability. They need to find acceptance again for what was once, they were *told*, unacceptable. That needs to be an important part of any INSET programme, because those less confident teachers *do* have a chance to redeem their own experience if they are prepared to explore again the uncharted territories with their younger pupils, who can offer an acceptance unavailable from some music teachers of the past. They can offer their teachers a delight in sound and freedom to experiment that contemporary classical composers, who are also rediscovering this area, often miss in the 'well-trained' choirs that perform their music. That freedom to experiment is often 'taught out' of pupils, and we must devise ways of keeping this alive, while at the same time teaching the more defined skills. If the composing area is kept alive in the curriculum (and if it includes vocal improvisation), this should happen. The area of singing is clearly delineated in the End of Key Stage Statements on performing. At the end of Key Stage 1, pupils are asked to be able to 'sing in a group a variety of songs' while at the end of Key Stage 2 they should be able to 'sing and play, with control of the sounds made, music from various times, places and cultures'.

The progression here is clear in terms of control, with a freedom implied at Key Stage 1, but this is not the experience of many of our generalist teachers and they will need help to make that progression themselves.

Cross-curricular opportunities
It is good to see references to movement and dance in the music document, both in the statutory Programmes of Study and in the examples given in the non-statutory Levels of Attainment. It is a pity that, although in the Programme of Study for Key Stage 1, children are to be taught how to 'respond to the musical elements, character and mood of a piece of music by means of movement and other forms of expression (eg dance, paint a picture)' this is not reflected in the appraising End of Key Stage 1 Statement which states '...listen attentively to a variety of music and identify its main elements... use simple terms to talk about music they have listened to, performed and composed.' I trust that the suggested dancing and painting in the Programme of Study is included in the verb 'identify' but regret that it was not spelled out more clearly.

In the Programme of Study for Key Stage 2, pupils are encouraged to 'relate musical activities to other work done in school, eg, for a medieval history project, perform songs and accompanied dances of the period'. And in Level 2 of composing, a suggestion for a project is to 'create a music pattern to match a movement pattern.' This is, in my experience, a very successful project.

Such suggestions clearly show the awareness of the centrality of topic work to the primary school day. In a chapter entitled 'exploring cross-curricular opportunities', the links with English, history, geography, mathematics, religious education, science and technology, and Welsh are explored in more detail. Perhaps more useful still is Annex F which identifies Attainment Targets in other areas which can be met in, and through, musical activities. In an age where Levels of Attainment in a variety of areas are proliferating with alarming speed to impossible proportions, the ability to fulfil a number of requirements in the same activity is essential and I do hope that this Annex will be preserved in literature supporting the statutory documents. So, in fulfilling Attainment Level 5 of performing – 'plan and present performance for a variety of audiences' – pupils could also be fulfilling two parts of English Level of Attainment 5:

> (c) use language to convey information and ideas effectively in a straightforward situation
> (d) contribute to the planning of, and participate in, a group presentation.

The references to music in the history document are highlighted and it is suggested that music could support parts of the geography area like Attainment Target 3 (physical geography) in which '...pupils should demonstrate their increasing knowledge of: (i) weather and climate (the atmosphere); (ii) rivers, river basins, sea and oceans (the hydrosphere); (iii) landform (the lithosphere); (iv) animals, plants and soils (the biosphere); and Level 3 (c), identify and describe a familiar landscape feature.'

A project in Tillman, *Forty Music Games to Make and Play*, based on Smetana's tone poem 'Vltava' which describes musically the course of the River Moldau from its source to the sea, could be an imaginative way of fulfilling this. Pupils create a piece entitled 'The River' which can be performed perhaps with dance, and listen critically to Smetana's work, comparing their own work with his. I hope that, in the area of geography, too, teachers will interpret the verb 'identify' more broadly than by simply using words.

Music and mathematics have traditionally attracted similar people and it is suggested that, for Attainment Target 2, 'numbers can be explored by singing counting songs or talking about "quarters" and "halves" in terms of duration of sounds.'

The requirement in science at Level 1 to 'observe familiar materials and events' clearly overlaps with composing Level 1, which encompasses 'sounds from a variety of sources, and includes silence.'

Perhaps not surprisingly, music is specified in the Attainment Targets for Welsh in which in Attainment Target 1 in the Programme of Study for Key Stage 1 pupils might be 'responding to sensory stimuli, eg listening to music, ...reciting, singing songs and rhymes learned by memory.' Similar links can be made in the area of discussing, as in English.

It is a pity that the art and PE (including dance) Final Documents were not available at the time of the writing of the music document. This precluded more detailed work on combined arts projects. The close link between dance and music is suggested in the linking of rhythmical grasp with movement, the idea of dance as a stimulus for composing, the use of music as a stimulus for dance and the suggestion that music and dance can be 'created simultaneously in an organic process'. A good project for 11-year-olds – creating a movement or dance sequence simultaneously with the music – can vary from work movements generating a song, or a piece of machinery with allied sounds, to disco style pieces with sounds created on an electronic keyboard. Music theatre pieces are also a delight to create, for the drama intensifies the understanding of music's expressive elements. Pupils' understanding of such forms as the musical and opera can be enhanced by this experience.

In the technology document there are specific references to music, such as 'Programmes of Study for Key Stage 1: Pupils should be taught to know that it is not always necessary to use the computer keyboard in order to produce information, for example, by using an overlay keyboard to select musical phrases.' The clear links with the composing area can be of great benefit to generalists with more confidence in the subject of technology than in music, especially at Key Stage 2 where 'Pupils should be taught to use information technology to organize ideas in written, pictorial, symbolic and aural forms.' The development of this field could be of great value in the area of composing specified under the End of Key Stage 2 Statement: 'Pupils should be able to create and store compositions, demonstrating an understanding of signs, symbols and cues.'

It is in this area of composing and the first statement in the area of performing that the role of musical notation is tightened up in this document as compared with the Interim Report. Techniques like that just described in the field of information technology will help, and paragraph 7.9 handles this sensitive subject gently, with all sorts of notational techniques being opened up:

We use the word notation to refer to any means of expressing the elements of music in written form. Young children acquire an awareness of musical elements (for example, high and low, quiet and loud, long and short) through repeated sound making and listening. In the early stages, teachers may use a three-dimensional object or objects to represent a sound or a pattern of sounds. This can lead to the use of graphic notation, in which elements such as exact pitch may not be precisely identified. Similarly, the density of a texture can be indicated by the thickness of a line, and differences in timbre by the use of different colours. *(Para. 7.9)*

This is followed, however, with a much firmer paragraph which means that there will certainly need to be some specialist help for generalist teachers between Key Stages 1 and 2:

> Through such improvisation and discovery, children can come to recognise the need to notate the music they are making, and attempt to meet that need. Awareness of relative pitch may be reinforced by the use of hand signs (such as those used according to the principles of Curwen or Kodaly), and these in turn may lead to the use of letter names for pitches (some teachers use Sol-fa), or numbering system. Notational systems, including staff notation, can thus be approached through active music-making. We expect them to be introduced to all pupils by the time they start on Key Stage 3, bearing in mind that pupils generally acquire facility in performing from notation before they develop the skill and understanding needed to notate their own and others' compositions. This is qualified by a reference to oral traditions and other forms of notation like chord symbols, ending with an exhortation that: 'The learning of notation divorced from sound can be said to negate its function and to be an arid study unrelated to music itself.' *(Para. 7.11)*

I hope that this is sufficient to prevent the old mismanagement of the theoretical teaching of notation coming back, with rows of silent children in silent rooms filling bars with 'correct' but 'unmusical' note values in an experience that may have more to do with mathematics than music.

Four areas for specialist care

Chapter 11 addresses 'equal opportunities in music', starting with the statement:

> All pupils, regardless of ethnic and cultural origin, of gender, and of physical and mental ability, have the right to experience music. Indeed, we believe that music has a very special role to play in breaking down barriers between pupils and realising potential within them. *(Para. 11.1)*

The chapter identifies four areas for special care: cultural heritage and diversity, sex and gender, music for children with special educational needs and the needs of the musically very able. It is a strong statement in this respect. The section on gender ends:

> It is important that teachers should monitor the engagement of both boys and girls in musical activities to ensure that choices are based on genuine musical preferences. At the primary level, for example, both girls and boys

should be given the opportunity to play large, loud instruments (drums, cymbals, mini basses); and at the secondary level, teachers might check that the composers studied and mentioned are not exclusively male.

There is a great deal of wisdom from current and recent projects, like the involvement of community groups in the area of cultural diversity, which states: '(e) relations and friends may be willing to bring into the school, and share with pupils, their particular enthusiasms, skills, instruments and recordings.'

Much work has been done throughout the document on the balance between various musical idioms in the light of much criticism of the Interim Document. The Programmes of Study include the following paragraph:

> Pupils should perform and listen to music in a variety of genres and styles, from different periods and cultures. The repertoire for this purpose should be chosen by teachers in the light of their pupils' needs, background and stage of musical development. It should, however, be a broad one, designed to extend and enrich pupils' musical experience; it should reflect musical trends and influences, and include reference to composers and performers who have proved influential in shaping and refining the language of music; and it should include a balanced selection of examples of works from all of the following categories:
> * the European 'classical' tradition, from its earliest roots to the present day;
> * folk and popular music;
> * music of the countries and regions of the British Isles;
> * other musical traditions and cultures.

Although not particularly clear, this is a useful checklist for schools and provides a bridge between those in favour of maintaining the indigenous culture (whatever that may be) and those more at ease with cultural diversity. Examples drawn from a variety of cultures are included in the Programmes of Study but more explicitly those for Key Stages 3 and 4.

There is a useful and comprehensive list of pointers to exceptional potential:

> Exceptional potential may be demonstrated in too many ways to be listed conclusively. Some pointers include:
> * 'getting it right' first time;
> * exceptional quickness in memorizing music;
> * an instinctive rhythmic perception;

- the possession of an acute sense of pitch;
- a spontaneous and authentic creative impulse in performing and composing, possibly shown by exceptionally fast progress through the levels of one or both of these Attainment Target areas;
- exceptional and sustained inner motivation for making music;
- exceptional affinity to an instrument, shown, for example, by an unwillingness to be parted from it or by a particular ease of physical response to it;
- an individual expressive personality, demonstrated, perhaps, by a natural tendency to shape a musical phrase sensitively;
- a high level of musical activity carried on out of school, such as spontaneous composing, an enthusiastic response to private instrumental tuition, or recognized expertise in a local band or group rehearsing on their own initiative.

For these musically very able pupils of all ages it is essential that some form of instrumental teaching is available. Chapters 13 and 14 not only identify, but stress, the role of the music support service:

> The advisory role of the support teacher in primary schools is likely to assume a greater importance as a result of the implementation of our recommendations; and a significant increase in demand for this type of support is anticipated. *(Para. 15.15)*

Instrumental teaching

Only recorder playing is specifically identified at Key Stage 2 and it is clear that the Working Party has tried hard to walk the fine line between getting these references in the statutory parts of the document to cement the place of instrumental services in an age which appears to be steadily eroding them and being realistic about what might be provided under LMS. There is clearly the implication that instrumental teachers need to be more integrated into classroom work and there will need to be imaginative work on how to make their help available to the maximum number of pupils.

There is a clear awareness that, at Key Stage 2, primary teachers will need more musical expertise than has previously been expected and an encouragement to increase the availability of a specialism in music in primary initial teacher training courses. The content of this is spelled out in some detail:

- basic training in the use of the voice and in singing, to give teachers the confidence and skill to lead pupils' singing and teach them effectively;
- training in organizing practical activities designed to encourage pupils to listen and respond to music through recognizing its elements, and to explore sounds and improvise in simple ways, using simple percussion instruments correctly;
- training in basic recording techniques; and, at Key Stage 2:
- additional training in ways of enabling pupils to recognize musical elements used in a variety of musical styles; and in the techniques of singing, directing, and playing a range of simple instruments;
- additional training in methods of simple composition, within various scales and structures; and an introduction to various forms of notation. *(Para. 15.6)*

Various INSET suggestions are made with a stress on classroom-based work in the hands of a music co-ordinator or advisory teacher or consultant. These could be shared between a cluster of schools. There is a suggestion that the specialist expertise from a neighbouring secondary school could be used. A collaboration between schools, colleges offering degrees in education including students, lecturers and teachers could benefit everyone. Music specialist students on a primary BEd degree course have musical expertise, classroom teachers have the teaching skills and experience and a lecturer experienced in delivering INSET can act as a link between the two. The students can be trained in college, and then work with teachers in the schools in a mutually beneficial enterprise, in schemes such as those being developed at places like King Alfred's College, Winchester.

Generalist teachers are going to need help and I trust that a glossary of terms will be included in the Statutory Orders with some clarifications of the muddles that exist in the present one over musical elements and form.

Assessment

In the area of assessment there is much helpful advice – it should be practical, part of the classroom process, formative and summative, include participation in group work and the widest practicable range of types of tasks and settings; it should involve self assessment that is based on clearly understood, reasonable and unambiguous criteria; it should be continuous and cumulative, involving music support staff; and it should include recognition of participation in extra-curricular activity.

Perhaps most vital is that it is part of the classroom process. My son recently had to do a forward roll alone in front of the class for a PE assessment. It was then that I realized that we could repeat the same public experience of failure if in music we were to settle for scaled down versions of Associated Board aural tests as a means of assessment. Assessment has got to be by means of projects in which all can be involved meaningfully, whatever their ability and skill (eg a group composition called 'A peaceful Lake' in which it is possible to see and hear that Pauline has reached Attainment Level 2b in performing, being able to: 'perform patterns of rhythm and pitch, by ear and from symbols', while in the same piece Tom demonstrates that he is at Level 1c at which he is able to: 'produce simple sound patterns with voice, body and instruments.').

The onus lies on the teacher to identify these levels and this will need extensive INSET and support while each child contributes something of value to the project.

The UKCMET Committee on Examinations and Assessment in Music's response to the document (3) sets out possible tasks for Key Stages 1 and 2 (pp. 2–3)

Key Stage 1 (Age 7):
Pupils will be able to present and recognize a mood in sound.
Skills
Choosing and playing sounds to represent a mood.
Critical Appraisal
Judging the appropriateness of the sounds in representing the mood in relation to their own and other pupils' efforts.

Key Stage 2 (Age 11):
Pupils will be able to create and perform a piece based on repetitive patterns involving more than one instrument, (could include voice), either simultaneously or successively.
Skills
Creating a coherent piece, and performing it convincingly.
Critical Appraisal
Judging the successful use of the repetitive patterns in relation to their own and other pupils' work.

No longer an optional extra

Music can no longer be regarded as an optional extra. It is not a 'frill'. It is unique in the artistic area as a way of bringing people together (hence the centrality of singing to school assembly) and also in expressing areas of life that otherwise would find no outlet. It is the only temporal (needing a period of time in which to happen) non-verbal art apart from its closest ally, dance. The visual arts are initially taken in at a glance and drama requires words. As such, there will be some people who will only relate through music (and the history of many musical cultures is full of these) and some who will only find their way into other ways of relating through the music. In my days as a class teacher, I had a child in my class who was school-phobic. When he was in school, he was fairly happy in those areas of the curriculum where the work was largely individual, like language, maths and art. But in areas that required group co-operation, he remained firmly rooted to the wall – in dance, drama, games and gym – and obstinately refused to take any part. Only in the area of composing did he offer anything of himself, and this was a repeated drum beat (probably his own pulse), but it was always possible to fit this into a class composition somewhere. I believe that the measure to which he was able to relate to others in other ways as well by the end of the year, was the measure to which he was found a musical place in the group. If that had not been on offer he might never have found it.

With adequate INSET and support, the Final Document could herald an age in which no one will want or be able to call themselves unmusical. All will realize their right to 'musick' with others. We could redeem the mistakes of past music education and allow the musician which lies inside everyone to emerge and take flight.

References

Swanwick, K. (1979) *A Basis for Music Education*. NFER.

Swanwick, K. and Tillman, J. B. (1986) 'The sequence of musical development.' *British Journal of Music Education*. Vol. 3 No. 3 pp. 305–39.

Tillman, J. (1983) *Forty Music Games to Make and Play*. London and Basingstoke: Macmillan.

UK Council for Music Education and Training Committee on Assessment and Examinations in Music (1991) *Report on the Interim Document*.